IMPACT Learning

CHANDOS

INFORMATION PROFESSIONAL SERIES

Series Editor: Ruth Rikowski

(email: Rikowskigr@aol.com)

Chandos' new series of books is aimed at the busy information professional. They have been specially commissioned to provide the reader with an authoritative view of current thinking. They are designed to provide easy-to-read and (most importantly) practical coverage of topics that are of interest to librarians and other information professionals. If you would like a full listing of current and forthcoming titles, please visit www.chandospublishing.com.

New authors: we are always pleased to receive ideas for new titles; if you would like to write a book for Chandos, please contact Dr Glyn Jones on g.jones.2@elsevier.com or telephone +44 (0) 1865 843000.

IMPACT Learning

Librarians at the Forefront of Change in Higher Education

CLARENCE MAYBEE

CHANDOS
PUBLISHING

An imprint of Elsevier

Chandos Publishing is an imprint of Elsevier
50 Hampshire Street, 5th Floor, Cambridge, MA 02139, United States
The Boulevard, Langford Lane, Kidlington, OX5 1GB, United Kingdom

Notices

Knowledge and best practice in this field are constantly changing. As new research and experience broaden our understanding, changes in research methods, professional practices, or medical treatment may become necessary.

Practitioners and researchers must always rely on their own experience and knowledge in evaluating and using any information, methods, compounds, or experiments described herein. In using such information or methods they should be mindful of their own safety and the safety of others, including parties for whom they have a professional responsibility.

To the fullest extent of the law, neither the Publisher nor the authors, contributors, or editors, assume any liability for any injury and/or damage to persons or property as a matter of products liability, negligence or otherwise, or from any use or operation of any methods, products, instructions, or ideas contained in the material herein.

Library of Congress Cataloging-in-Publication Data
A catalog record for this book is available from the Library of Congress

British Library Cataloguing-in-Publication Data
A catalogue record for this book is available from the British Library

ISBN: 978-0-08-102077-7 (print)
ISBN: 978-0-08-102103-3 (online)

For information on all Chandos publications
visit our website at https://www.elsevier.com/books-and-journals

Working together
to grow libraries in
developing countries

www.elsevier.com • www.bookaid.org

Publisher: Glyn Jones
Acquisition Editor: Glyn Jones
Editorial Project Manager: Naomi Robertson
Production Project Manager: Swapna Srinivasan
Cover Designer: Greg Harris

Typeset by SPi Global, India

DEDICATION

This book is dedicated to my wife April, who inspires me every day.

CONTENTS

FOREWORD

It is with the greatest pleasure that I pen this introduction to *IMPACT Learning: Librarians at the Forefront of Change in Higher Education.*

Learning lies at the heart of personal development, change, progress, innovation, creativity, and growth. At all times people are using information to learn, and here learning means changing, modifying, and adjusting some way in which we experience the world, an interpretation of learning arising from extensive educational research into the experience of learning (Marton, 2014; Marton & Booth, 1997). Of course, people do not just use information to learn, they always use information to learn something. This is a cornerstone of informed learning (Bruce, 2008), also derived from the same strand of educational research.

Informed learning highlights the importance of appreciating the diverse ways in which learners experience information literacy and what they are learning; as well as proposing "… ways of helping students learn content through the process of effective information use" (Bruce, 2000, p. 7). At its heart informed learning is about being an integral part of the learning agenda, going beyond integrating information literacy into curriculum, to transforming approaches to learning in ways that empower learners for their academic, professional and personal futures. We therefore need to design learning in ways that encourage learners to adopt learning patterns that involve explicit attention to information use, adopting a design philosophy that Biggs (1997) refers to as "constructive alignment".

In *IMPACT Learning,* Clarence Maybee continues this tradition, revealing the critical importance of connecting with evolving higher education directions and agendas through partnering in university wide transformative developmental programming for enriching learning. Not only are such programs transforming design processes, the processes designed and embedded by the Instruction Matters: Purdue Academic Course Transformation (IMPACT) team are also transforming learning… building strong connections between information use and "content" learning, facilitating reflection on information use and its role in "content" learning.

The place of information use in the learning process is recognized by discipline educators and other members of the learning design team. It is also brought into focus and made explicit to students who are invited to engage in a reflective journey of interpreting the value and importance of effective information use in their discipline or professional domain.

In this volume, Clarence Maybee reveals how research and practice can move forward together. He explores the application of these ideas in very practical ways revealing how the principles might be adopted elsewhere. IMPACT is emerging as a sustainable model from which key lessons can be learned and applied to other formal contexts. Throughout Clarence foreshadows, and reveals in the final chapter, his vision for Informed Learning Design—a research-driven practical approach to designing learning experiences that value and harness associated information experiences as a critical strategy for transformational, learner focused information literacy education.

Clarence's thought and application in IMPACT Learning has powerful potential to keep librarians and other educators at the forefront of change in higher education; as well as powerful potential for the education of lifelong learners. It deserves careful consideration by the entire higher education community.

C. Bruce

James Cook University, Townsville, QLD, Australia

REFERENCES

Biggs, J. (1997). What the student does: Teaching for enhanced learning. *Higher Education Research and Development*, 18(1), 55–76.

Bruce, C. S. (2000). Introduction. In C. S. Bruce & P. C. Candy (Eds.), *Information literacy around the world: Advances in programs and research*. Wagga Wagga, N.S.W.: Charles Sturt University.

Bruce, C. S. (2008). *Informed learning*. Chicago, IL: American Library Association.

Marton, F. (2014). *Necessary conditions for learning*. New York: Routledge.

Marton, F., & Booth, S. (1997). *Learning and awareness*. Mahwah, NJ: Lawrence Erlbaum.

PART 1

Fostering Learning Through Librarianship

CHAPTER 1

Introduction

Contents

Abstract

This chapter presents the main premise of this book: that information literacy efforts need to address the ways that information is used in various learning contexts. Informed learning, which emphasizes "learning" as the key outcome of using information, is suggested as a more appropriate approach for addressing information literacy in higher education. The chapter outlines the three parts of this book. Part 1 focuses on the need for information literacy efforts to focus on enabling students to learn to use information as part of engaging with course content. Part 2 describes how academic librarians at Purdue University have adopted an informed learning approach to integrating information literacy into courses when participating in a course redesign program. Part 3 offers three essential elements that may guide academic librarians' informed learning efforts at other campuses.

Keywords: Information literacy, Informed learning, Higher education, Academic librarians, Educational initiatives.

In the report that famously introduced the concept of information literacy, Zukowski (1974) concluded with a call for education for "…all citizens in the use of the information tools now available as well as those in the development…" (p. 27). Heeding this call, academic libraries have taken the lead in creating information literacy programming on higher education campuses. Over the last several decades, academic libraries have expanded their educational role by developing information literacy curricula and new positions and policies. Academic librarians have cultivated new professional skills related to pedagogy, instructional design, and assessment. In the United States, this work has largely been guided by the Association for College and Research Libraries (ACRL) through their efforts to define information literacy (ACRL, 2000, 2015), and support academic libraries in developing programs (ACRL, 2000, 2003). A testament to the efforts of the library community, today information literacy is included in educational standards documents across the Western industrialized world (Bradley, 2013).

In spite of these achievements, the academic library community currently faces major challenges in advancing information literacy in higher education. Guided largely by ACRL, academic libraries adopted a definition of information literacy that emphasizes discrete information skills. Typically taught by academic librarians, the information skills approach to information literacy in higher education focuses on creating learning activities and courses to cover the new content of information skills. An information literacy course taught as part of a general education curriculum may have students learn to search databases, recognize types of information (e.g., peer-reviewed articles, news, government documents), evaluate sources by specific criteria, and properly cite sources. In learning specific information skills, academic libraries' efforts do not encompass important educational aims, such as teaching students to use information within disciplinary contexts, or making students aware of the social and political aspects of information production and use.

New models have been proposed that place the learning of information skills and concepts into broader contexts. ACRL's (2015) *Framework for Information Literacy for Higher Education* is one such model intended to address some of these concerns. For example, the *Framework* emphasizes communal aspects of scholarship, extending evaluative criteria to have learners consider how a community construes the authority of a piece of information. However, other new models go further, calling for a closer connection between information literacy and the societal or professional learning goals that are part of a higher education curriculum (e.g., Bruce, 2008; Lloyd, 2010; Whitworth, 2014). Accomplishing this requires that students use information within the broader learning context of the disciplinary classroom. As such, these approaches require changes to the current higher education information literacy practices developed by academic libraries.

Drawing from information literacy scholarship, the argument set forth in this book is that academic libraries need to reconceptualize information literacy to make it central to their institution's mission for learning. Rather than thinking of it as a set of prescribed information skills that students must acquire, informed learning (Bruce, 2008) is an approach that emphasizes "learning" as the key outcome of using information. This approach is a more appropriate guide to fostering information literacy outcomes in higher education. Recognizing that what students are able to learn is influenced by how students use information when learning (Maybee, Bruce, Lupton, & Rebmann, 2017), informed learning focuses on having students engage with information intentionally (Bruce, 2008). For example, a teacher of a language and gender course who was frustrated with students finding sources that aligned with their preexisting views of a topic decided to have the students trace the scholarly literature to map the evolution of a the topic (Maybee et al., 2017). In line with the teacher's goals for learning, changing how they used information allowed the students to learn different things about the topic they chose to investigate than if they had been assigned the typical research paper.

Adopting an informed learning perspective in higher education would require changing how we approach information literacy education. Academic librarians, with their knowledge of how information is used to learn in higher education learning environments, would continue to be key actors in developing information literacy education. However, they would need to work more closely with classroom teachers to advocate for, and design, learning experiences that integrate information literacy into course curricula.

Illuminating the need for changes in how academic libraries approach information literacy, this book also provides an example, outlining how the Purdue University Libraries adopt such an approach to integrate information literacy into undergraduate courses on their campus. Purdue is a large research university in the Midwestern United States, with over 30,000 undergraduate students and 9000 graduate students. Purdue Libraries is part of a group that spearheaded "Instruction Matters: Purdue Academic Course Transformation" (IMPACT), an initiative to redesign large foundational courses to make them more student-centered, by shifting away from a lecture-based model to create learning environments in which students are actively and fully engaged (Barr & Tagg, 1995). Across thirteen weekly meetings, teachers work with librarians, instructional designers, and technologists to make courses more active and engaging. Correlated with a small, but statically significant, increase in grades, 79.4% of the 225 courses redesigned between 2011 and 2016 were perceived by students to be student-centered.

In addition to fostering student-centered learning, Purdue Libraries recognizes that the IMPACT program provides an opportunity to integrate information literacy into foundational courses. Rather than advocating the value of information skills generally, librarians work with teachers in IMPACT to identify how learning to use information in specific ways fosters content learning outcomes. This book outlines a number of key aspects of advancing the integration of information literacy used by Purdue librarians when working with the teachers participating in IMPACT.

Teaching and learning initiatives such as IMPACT, where higher education teachers are applying new pedagogic ideas to course curricula, provide tremendous opportunities for academic librarians to advance informed learning. For example, a statistics teacher who participated in the IMPACT program worked with a librarian and an information technologist to design an assignment in which students evaluate statistics they encounter in the news. To encourage the application of critical evaluation in real-life settings, the assignment has students discuss their conclusions with other students in posts to a Facebook-like social media tool (Gundlach, Maybee, & O'Shea, 2015). A technology teacher worked with a librarian to have students engage with information from both scholarly articles and original research data to inform their designs. While both are examples of informed learning, the first draws disciplinary methods of evaluating information into an everyday situation (Facebook discussions), while the second example prepares students to use information as they might in their future professional lives.

Drawing from Purdue Libraries' experiences of partnering with teachers in the IMPACT program, the book outlines an approach that academic librarians can use to integrate information literacy into course curricula on their campuses. Adopting the approach described throughout this book will place academic libraries' information literacy efforts in a central role in contributing to the societal and professional learning goals being called for in higher education.

1.1 PURPOSE OF THIS BOOK

This book is for information literacy librarians, researchers, and teachers who are interested in addressing the situated and critical aspects of information literacy in formal educational settings. Grounded in scholarship, the book provides an approach to guide academic libraries' efforts to integrate information literacy into higher education curricula. Drawing from efforts to integrate information literacy into course curricula through involvement in an innovative teaching and learning initiative, the book offers practical guidance concerning how to advance this approach in higher education. With the greater goal of empowering higher education students to use information to learn and accomplish things within the various contexts in which they work and live, the book aims to inform information literacy practices in higher education.

1.2 STRUCTURE OF THE BOOK

This book is comprised of three parts. Part 1 describes the need for information literacy education to allow students to practice using information in the contexts in which they are learning. It proposes teaching and learning initiatives as a target for librarians to focus their efforts to integrate information literacy into course curricula. To provide an example of how academic libraries can leverage such initiatives to integrate information literacy into disciplinary courses, Part 2 describes Purdue Libraries' partnership to create a course redesign program to foster student-centered learning that integrates information literacy into courses. Part 3 draws from lessons learned from the Purdue Libraries' experiences with the IMPACT program to offer three essential elements to guide efforts to integrate information literacy into the disciplinary classroom. This part also outlines the development needed for academic librarians to support them in the pursuit of such efforts.

1.2.1 Part 1: Fostering Learning Through Librarianship

Part 1 sets the stage for the second and third parts of the book by drawing from scholarship to outline ways to advance information literacy in higher education. Chapter 2 examines information literacy education and research, suggesting that current information literacy practices in higher education overemphasize learning discrete information skills at the expense of students practicing using information in specific contexts. Informed learning, an approach developed by Christine Bruce (2008), is presented as an alternative to the current information literacy practices in higher education. Viewing learning as a major outcome of using information, informed learning offers a pedagogic approach that enables the creation of learning environments in which students become aware of new ways of using information within the context of learning in a disciplinary course.

Chapter 3 outlines how teaching and learning initiatives on college and university campuses provide opportunities for academic librarians to work to integrate information literacy into course curricula. The chapter also highlights aspects of collaboration that can support academic librarians in their efforts to integrate information literacy into courses using an informed learning approach.

1.2.2 Part 2: Course Development at Purdue: A Case for Fostering Learning Through Information Literacy

Part 2 describes Purdue Libraries' involvement in the IMPACT program, an educational initiative at Purdue that focuses on creating transformative learning experiences for undergraduate students. The purpose of Part 2 is to offer an example of how academic libraries can integrate information literacy into disciplinary courses. Each chapter in Part 2 of this book contains a profile written by a librarian or classroom teacher, in which they describe their experience working with the IMPACT program.

Chapter 4 provides an overview of IMPACT, describes Purdue Libraries' interest, and aims in participating in the creation and development of the program. It also outlines the role of individual librarians as team members working with classroom teachers and staff from other units at Purdue to redesign courses. Chapter 5 describes the approach Purdue librarians have taken in their work on IMPACT teams, recognizing the need not to advocate for information literacy until a pedagogic issue is identified in which learning may be enhanced by students using information more intentionally. Librarians' efforts are supported through the use of the backward design (Wiggins & McTighe, 2005), an instructional design model that provides a shared structure to discuss aspects of the course.

Chapter 6 describes classroom teachers' views of information literacy, including the findings from a study conducted at Purdue of teachers who had completed the IMPACT program. The teachers in the study reported having students use information, either in general or discipline-specific ways, to learn about course content. Chapter 7 provides vignettes highlighting partnerships among teachers, librarians, and others to create informed learning in courses redesigned through the IMPACT program. Three of the four vignettes outline informed learning assignments, such as a statistical literacy course in which students critically discuss statistical information found in the news, and changes to an assignment in a biology course designed to make information literacy more relevant to students. The chapter concludes with a description of a new research project conducted at Purdue to determine the relationship between information literacy, student perceptions of motivation, and course grades.

Chapter 8 outlines how librarians have drawn from educational theories and models they are introduced to through their work in the IMPACT program to develop new information literacy tools. The last chapter in Part 2, Chapter 9 outlines lessons learned from Purdue Libraries' participation in the IMPACT program. One lesson learned was that advocating for information literacy in and of itself is unproductive. The second lesson learned was that integrating information literacy into courses required that the librarians focus on issues or challenges faced by a classroom teacher, and when appropriate, introduce information literacy as a potential solution. The third lesson learned was that the librarians participating in IMPACT teams needed to be open to a broad range of possible ways that a teacher and students might construe what is useful information and how it may be used in the learning process.

1.2.3 Part 3: Reenvisioning Information Literacy Education

Part 3 focuses on applying the ideas introduced in Parts 1 and 2 to advance the integration of information literacy into course curricula at other institutions. Chapter 10 introduces three essentials for working with departments and faculty to integrate information literacy into courses. The first of the three is that academic librarians must focus on student learning when working with classroom teachers to integrate information literacy. The second is targeting high-profile educational initiatives as a place where teachers may be open to new educational ideas, such as information literacy. Lastly, academic librarians should use consulting approaches that focus on creating shared goals when partnering to integrate information literacy into course curricula.

Chapter 11 outlines the knowledge and skills required by academic librarians to participate in educational initiatives on their campuses. Existing professional development options are identified as possible ways of bridging potential gaps. Chapter 12 concludes the book with a call to change information literacy practices in higher education by adopting an informed learning approach utilizing the strategies outlined in the previous chapters.

REFERENCES

ACRL. (2000). *Information literacy competency standards for higher education*. Chicago, IL: Association of College and Research Libraries.

ACRL. (2003, revised 2012). Characteristics of programs of information literacy that illustrate best practices: A guideline. ACRL. Retrieved from http://www.ala. org/acrl/standards/characteristics.

ACRL. (2015). Framework for information literacy for higher education. Association of College and Research Libraries Retrieved from http://www.ala.org/acrl/standards/ilframework.

Barr, R. B., & Tagg, J. (1995). From teaching to learning: A new paradigm for undergraduate education. *Change, 27*(6), 12–25.

Bradley, C. (2013). Information literacy in the programmatic university accreditation standards of select professions in Canada, the United States, the United Kingdom, and Australia. *Journal of Information Literacy, 7*(1), 44–68.

Bruce, C. S. (2008). *Informed Learning*. Chicago, IL: American Library Association.

Gundlach, E., Maybee, C., & O'Shea, K. (2015). Statistical literacy social media project for the masses. *The Journal of Faculty Development, 29*(2), 71–80.

Lloyd, A. (2010). *Information literacy landscapes: Information literacy in education, workplace and everyday contexts*. Oxford: Chandos.

Maybee, C., Bruce, C. S., Lupton, M., & Rebmann, K. (2017). Designing rich information experiences to shape learning outcomes. *Studies in Higher Education, 42*(12), 2373–2388.

Whitworth, A. (2014). *Radical information literacy: Reclaiming the political heart of the IL movement*. Burlington: Elsevier Science.

Wiggins, G. P., & McTighe, J. (2005). *Understanding by design* (2nd ed.). Alexandria, VA: Association for Supervision and Curriculum Development.

Zurkowski, P. G. (1974). *The information service environment relationships and priorities* [Related Paper No. 5]. National Commission on Libraries and Information Science, National Program for Library and Information Services.

CHAPTER 2

From Information Literacy to Informed Learning

Contents

Abstract

This chapter reviews the literature on information literacy in higher education. Information literacy can be categorized as (1) functional, (2) situated, or (3) critical. Information skills are associated with the functional approach, which is the approach most often utilized in information literacy efforts in higher education. The situated approach emphasizes the role of information in disciplinary or professional contexts. A critical approach aims to make students aware of the social and political aspects of information production and use. Informed learning is put forward as an approach in which information literacy is an intrinsic part of the learning goals that underpin higher education course curricula, and thus would align with broader educational goals aimed at enculturating learners into disciplinary or professional roles, as well as providing them with a critical lens through which to challenge cultural and societal conventions.

Keywords: Approaches to information literacy, Information skills, Situated information literacy, Critical information literacy, Informed learning.

2.1 INTRODUCTION

Learners need to practice using information within a context, such as a discipline or professional learning situation (Bruce, 2008; Lloyd, 2010). The Association of College and Research Libraries (ACRL) suggest that academic librarians and classroom teachers are both responsible for information literacy education (ACRL, 2000, 2015).

So, what is the role of academic librarians in teaching higher education students to use information in the context of the higher education classroom? Cowan (2014) has argued that while librarians drew needed attention to information literacy in the past, their role in educating students should now be handed off to classroom teachers. This assertion does not leverage the knowledge of and expertise in information literacy built up by academic librarians over the past four decades. Nevertheless, that Cowan could take such a position does suggest that it is time for the academic library community to examine their role in information literacy education.

Recognizing that there is more than one approach to addressing this challenge, this chapter reviews different ideas and events surrounding information literacy. The review identifies gaps that exist between what students may learn through standard information literacy practices adopted in higher education and other approaches to information literacy. The chapter concludes by suggesting that informed learning (Bruce, 2008), which emphasizes learning to use information should occur in the context of learning course content, offers an approach to information literacy that better aligns with higher education goals for learning.

2.2 THE BURGEONING OF INFORMATION LITERACY

Information literacy developed as a solution to the problem of the ubiquity of information caused by advances in information technology (Zurkowski, 1974). It developed in tandem to several educational ideas that focused on providing students with learning experiences intended for them to engage deeply and more personally with the content they were learning. A key idea, still a major focus of educational development in higher education, was student-centered learning, which argues for a change in the role of teachers from "disseminators" of content to "facilitators" of learning (Barr and Tagg, 1995). Student-centered learning highlights active engagement as essential for learning.

Definitions of information literacy adopted in higher education to guide instructional efforts were not particularly concerned with progressive views of teaching and learning. Instead, they focused on changes related to how information is produced and disseminated. Therefore, the definitions of information literacy adopted in higher education focused on perceived changes in how information was encountered and needed to be managed by individuals. An early document that heavily influenced the construction of information literacy in higher education was a report by the American Library Association's (ALA) Presidential Committee on Information Literacy (ALA, 1989). The report, which described information literacy as desired skills, defined an information literate person as:

1. knowing when they have a need for information,
2. identifying information required to address a given problem or issue,
3. finding needed information and evaluating the information,
4. organizing the information, and
5. using the information effectively to solve the problem or issue at hand (ALA, 1989).

The information skills identified by ALA (1989) as being part of information literacy were recognized at the time by experts from the field of education (Doyle, 1992). Using a method called the Delphi Technique, Doyle had educators select and prioritize a list of information skills. The outcome of this study was a more detailed list defining an information literate person as someone who:

- recognizes the need for information;
- recognizes that accurate and complete information is the basis for intelligent decision-making;
- formulates questions based on information needs;
- identifies potential sources of information;
- develops successful search strategies;
- accesses sources of information, including computer-based and other technologies;
- evaluates information;
- organizes information for practical application;
- integrates new information into an existing body of knowledge; and
- uses information in critical thinking and problem-solving (Doyle, 1992).

In academic libraries in the 1980s and 1990s, the information skills considered to be a part of information literacy were associated with the bibliographic instruction training librarians provided, which focused on teaching students how to identify information and techniques for finding it (Reichel & Arp, 1990; Snavely & Cooper, 1997). Some considered bibliographic instruction to be a subset of information literacy, which was more encompassing as it included evaluating information as well as finding it.

The resources and services of the academic library were a primary focus of discussions on information literacy. In their book, *Information Literacy: Revolution in the Library*, Breivik and Gee (1989) advocated for what they termed "library-based learning." Library-based learning requires students to engage with information via the library rather than through course materials provided by the teacher. The approach is notable for its times, because it advocated for independent engagement with information rather than reinforcing the dominant approach, in which the teachers were the primary access point for students to encounter scholarly materials.

Associated with concepts such as "learning to learn," process models introduced in the 1980s and 1990s emphasized that learners engage in various stages of a linear process comprised of information skills (Eisenberg & Berkowitz, 1990; Eisenberg, Lowe, & Spitzer, 2004; Irving, 1985; Kuhlthau, 1993; Pappas & Tepe, 2002; Stripling & Pitts, 1988). Kuhlthau (1993) developed the Information Search Process (ISP), which outlined six steps students engage in when conducting literature-based research for college assignments:

1. task initiation,
2. topic selection,
3. prefocus exploration,
4. focus formulation,
5. information collection, and
6. search closure.

Drawn from a study of students engaged in an assignment that required finding and using information sources (Kuhlthau, 1993), the ISP model differs from other models by describing how students feel as they engage in the various steps of the process. While not concerned with the learning of disciplinary content per se, the focus of the ISP model on the affective aspects of learning represented an important step towards acknowledging the experiences of the student in learning to use information.

The publishing of the *Information Literacy Competency Standards for Higher Education* by the Association of College and Research Libraries (ACRL, 2000) solidified an information skills-focused definition of information literacy in higher education in the United States. Drawing from the ALA (1989) definition, the *Standards* describe an information literate student as being able to:

- determine the extent of information needed,
- access the needed information effectively and efficiently,
- evaluate information and its sources critically and incorporate selected information into one's knowledge base,
- use information effectively to accomplish a specific purpose, and
- understand the economic, legal, and social issues surrounding the use of information, and access and use information ethically and legally (ACRL, 2000).

Between 2000 and 2015 (when they were rescinded), academic librarians used the *Standards* to develop and validate information literacy instruction and assessment efforts. The voluminous literature describing lessons, courses, tutorials, and projects framed by the *Standards* is indicative of their tremendous influence upon information literacy teaching practice in higher education.

2.3 AN ABUNDANCE OF NEW IDEAS ABOUT INFORMATION LITERACY

As considered by many measures, the advancement of information literacy in the form of information skills curricula is successful. In addition to the growth of dedicated staff and curricula on college campuses, a key indicator of success is the widespread influence of the *Standards* (ACRL, 2000). They have been used not only in framing the efforts of academic libraries, but also in guiding the development of other standards in the United States and elsewhere. The ACRL *Standards* have influenced standards developed to guide information literacy education in various disciplinary settings (ACRL, 2008, 2011a, 2011b, 2013) as well as general standards by library advocacy organizations in other westernized nations (Bundy, 2004; SCONUL, 2011). In addition, the ACRL (2000) *Standards* has informed other, nonlibrary, higher education advocacy, and oversight organizations in the United States. For example, the American Association of Colleges and Universities (AACU, 2009) developed an information literacy rubric to guide institutional efforts. Accrediting agencies, to varying degrees, have also provided lists of information skills to be included in higher education curricula (MSCHE, 2003, 2009; NEASC, 2005; WASC, 2008).

However, there are major criticisms of the information skills approach to information literacy. Information literacy, as with literacy generally, can be categorized as (1) functional, (2) situated, or (3) critical (Lupton & Bruce, 2010). Information skills are associated with the *functional* approach, which is the approach most often utilized in information literacy efforts in higher education. The *situated* approach emphasizes the role of information in specific contexts, such as disciplinary or professional settings. A *critical* approach to information literacy aims to make students aware of social and political aspects of information production and use. The critical approach, which focuses on empowering students to advance social change, is becoming more popular amongst academic librarians. Nevertheless, the academic library community has not widely adopted situated and critical approaches to information literacy into practice in higher education.

Why has the academic library community advanced a functional approach to information literacy education over a situated or critical approach? It is possible that creating a curriculum of information skills aligns better with the processes and structures already existing in higher education. That is, it may be easier to argue to administrators that learning information skills supports professional preparation, often construed as the primary purpose of higher education. Existing conventions in higher education lend themselves to thinking about information literacy as new content (comprised of information skills) that needs to be covered within a curriculum, whereas a situated or critical approach to information literacy might focus on new pedagogic techniques in which using information is directed towards learning (Bruce, 2008; Lupton, 2008). For example, students in an environmental studies course may be learning to use information to understand the practices in that field, or they may be planning to apply what they learned to advocate for changes in environmental policies and practices (Lupton, 2004).

Of course, there may be difficulties associated with developing new curricula. As teachers in higher education lament, there is seldom room to add more content to a course. Therefore, the content of information skills is often relegated to a single class period. However, advancing a situated or critical approach would emphasize using or applying information to learn or do something within a particular context. Enabling students to use information in the ways necessary for such an approach would require a type of collegial partnering that academic librarians may not have been prepared to embark on as they transitioned into teaching roles.

Regardless of what might have been feasible to advocate and introduce on higher education campuses in the 1980s and 1990s, there remains the greater concern as to what information literacy efforts intend to achieve, and which approach to information literacy will best enable those results. An analysis of information literacy documentation at higher education institutions revealed that academic libraries espouse the purpose of their programs as fostering learning, while implementation often focuses on teaching discrete skills (Kerr, 2009). While there may be challenges associated with adopting a situated or critical approach to information literacy, there may also be opportunities for learners, which are missed by not doing so.

The functional approach to information literacy assumes that students will be able to apply the information skills they acquire in higher education within the various settings in which they later learn and work. A situated approach emphases the ways in which information literacy is part of social and cultural practices (Lloyd, 2010). Lloyd and colleagues have conducted research to illuminate the information practices used in various contexts (e.g., Bonner & Lloyd, 2011, 2012; Lloyd, 2007, 2009; Lloyd, Kennan, Thompson, & Qayyum, 2013). From this perspective, learners need to practice using information in authentic, or nearly authentic, situations (Lloyd, 2010). Lloyd suggests that information literacy efforts in higher education are, at best, preparatory. Learning to use information within a context, such as a disciplinary or professional setting, only occurs once a student is working in that context.

To address its situated nature, Lloyd (2010) recommends using a *community of practice* approach, which emphasizes learning experiences where learners have a chance to observe and participate in the work of a group of practitioners (Brown & Duguid, 2000; Lave, 1996; Lave & Wenger, 1991). A practice community may be a profession, such as dentistry or law, but could also be a hobby or religion, or any group engaged in accomplishing a shared enterprise. In higher education, it is easy to see how experiences such as internships, service-learning, and undergraduate research, provide opportunities for integrating information literacy using a community of practice approach. However, courses taught in the classroom can also be designed to focus on aspects of enculturating students to use information within a disciplinary or professional context.

During the past decade, critical approaches to information literacy have been of increasing interest amongst information literacy researchers and practitioners (Tewell, 2015). Critical of the information skills approach to information literacy, researchers, and practitioners taking a critical approach to information literacy focus on making students aware of the sociopolitical and cultural forces that influence the creation, dissemination, and use of information (e.g., Elmborg, 2006; Kapitzke, 2003b; Pawley, 2003; Whitworth, 2014). Critical approaches to information literacy may be grounded in critical pedagogies put forth by scholars such as Pablo Freire (1993), Henry Giroux (1988), and numerous others, which aim to empower learners to overcome oppressive societal and educational structures. The book, *Critical Library Instruction: Theories and Methods,* discusses different aspects of a critical approach to information literacy, and includes practical methods for teaching from this perspective (Accardi, Drabinski, & Kumbier, 2010).

There is a significant difference between how the situated, critical, and foundational approaches focus on what is considered information. The information skills approach to information literacy applied in higher education tends to privilege printed texts, such as books and journal articles, as the authoritative information sources that students are taught to find and use (Kapitzke, 2003a). However, academic texts do not adequately prepare students to use information as they need to when learning and working within a particular context. Lloyd's research into the information practices of professionals has highlighted this. For example, her study with nurses reveals that nurses gather bodily information from their patients to make medical decisions (Bonner & Lloyd, 2011). In preparing students to become nurses, higher education information literacy efforts should also address this kind of information use.

Of course, ACRL (2000) has recognized shortcomings associated with the skills-centric approach to information literacy inherent in the *Standards*. As a result, they rescinded the *Standards* and put forth *The Framework for Information Literacy for Higher Education* (ACRL, 2015). Some have argued that the *Standards* are political documents, and that rescinding them diminished the ability of academic librarians to demonstrate the value of information literacy to institutional stakeholders, such as disciplinary faculty or administrators (Drabinski & Sitar, 2016; Jackman & Weiner, 2017). Drabinski and Sitar (2016) suggest that while the *Standards* empowered academic libraries to seek support for information literacy, they did not necessitate a curricular or pedagogical mandate.

The *Framework* (ACRL, 2015) addresses some of the criticisms of the information skills approach to information literacy espoused in the *Standards* (ACRL, 2000). The two theories that underpin the *Framework*, metaliteracy and threshold concepts theory, provide a broader definition of information literacy, while simultaneously providing specific targets for designing instruction. Metaliteracy aims to widen the scope of what is typically considered information literacy, by drawing together technology-related literacies, such as media and digital literacies (Jacobson & Mackey, 2011). Threshold concepts theory (Meyer & Land 2003) suggests that certain concepts pose barriers that are thresholds to be attained before further learning can occur. The findings from research using threshold concept theory to explore information literacy have been used to help design the *Framework* (Hofer, Brunetti, & Townsend, 2013). Filed in 2105, and adopted in 2016, the *Framework* contains six broad information-related concepts:

- Scholarship is a Conversation: scholarship is a sustained discourse within a community of scholars or thinkers, with new insights and discoveries occurring over time as a result of competing perspectives and interpretations.
- Research as Inquiry: research is iterative, and depends upon asking increasingly complicated questions whose answers develop new questions or lines of inquiry in any field.
- Format as Process: processes of developing information resources originate from different needs, motivations, values, conventions,

and practices, and result in different formats, but the underlying questions about the value of the information and its potential use are more significant than the physical packaging of the information source.

- Authority is Constructed and Contextual: information quality needed for a particular purpose varies, will use various types of evaluative criteria to match that purpose, and will trust the authority of that information with an attitude of informed skepticism, remaining open to new perspectives, additional voices, and changes in schools of thought.
- Searching as Exploration: searching and locating information involves defining an information need; knowing the universe of possible tools, collections, and repositories that may be useful in finding information; using appropriate search vocabularies and protocols to design specific search strategies or questions for using systems, databases, and other organized collections of knowledge; and refining and adjusting search strategies during the process of investigating the research topic.
- Information has Value: acknowledges that the creation of information and products derived from information requires a commitment of time, original thought, and resources respected by those seeking to use these products or create their own based on the work of others; information may be valued more or less highly based on its creator, its audience/consumer, or its message (ACRL, 2015).

The definition of information literacy provided by the *Framework* addresses some of the concerns of a situated or critical approach. The *Framework* speaks to issues related to using information in context, such as communal aspects of scholarship, and ideas related to the construction of authority. However, like the *Standards*, the *Framework* defines information literacy in a general way. That is, students are expected to learn concepts related to using information. Students are not intended to practice using information to learn or accomplish something within a particular context, such as a disciplinary learning environment. While they may be taught to apply a critical lens to the information they encounter, students are not applying that critical stance to effect change. The need to teach higher education students to use information as they will in the "real" world after college, continues to challenge academic libraries. To do so requires moving away from a definition of information literacy as learning information-related concepts, and instead, to provide students with ways of practicing using information for authentic, academic, disciplinary, professional, and personal purposes.

2.4 RETHINKING INFORMATION LITERACY IN HIGHER EDUCATION

Informed learning is a new way of approaching information literacy that can address its situated and critical natures. Introduced in a book published in 2008 (Bruce, 2008), informed learning was further elaborated on in journal articles authored by Christine Bruce and her colleagues (Bruce & Hughes, 2010; Bruce, Hughes, & Somerville, 2012; Bruce, Somerville, Stoodley, & Partridge, 2013; Hughes & Bruce, 2012). The central idea of informed learning is that students must learn to use information in the context of learning about a topic (Bruce, 2008). To achieve this aim, adopting an informed learning approach places information literacy in the disciplinary classroom. Advancing informed learning in higher education requires that academic librarians, with their knowledge of how students use information to learn, partner with teachers to integrate information literacy into course curricula.

Informed learning is associated with phenomenography, a research approach created and developed in reaction to research conducted between the 1960s and 1980s that used a variety of methods aimed at predicting students' capability or potential (Marton, Hounsell, & Entwistle, 1997). Phenomenographers believe that improving education requires understanding how students experience learning. Recognizing that learning requires students to become aware of aspects of the phenomenon they are studying, phenomenographers mapped the differences in students' awareness (Marton & Booth, 1997). For example, a study of 7- to 12-year-olds in different classes that were all studying cellular respiration and photosynthesis revealed that the younger students understood the function of oxygen and sugar in plants in the scientifically established way, whereas the older students did not (Vikström, 2008). The unexpected outcome resulted from a difference in the lessons the younger students received that allowed them to become aware of the phenomena as intended.

Researchers also recognized the importance of understanding the student experience of information literacy. In tandem with Bruce' seminal study of higher educators' experiences of information literacy, Swedish researcher Louise Limberg (1999, 2000) examined high school students' experiences of seeking information as well as how they experienced the social studies issue they investigated. Limberg's findings show a relationship between complex ways of finding information and the sophistication of which students understood their topic (Limberg, 2000). Aligned with educators' experiences (Bruce, 1997; Webber, Boon, & Johnston, 2005), studies of learners' experiences suggest that when information literacy focuses on learning about a topic, then information is used with more complexity (Andretta, 2012; Locke, 2009; Lupton, 2004, 2008, Maybee, 2006, 2007; Parker, 2006).

When information literacy focuses on learning about a topic, it may also be associated with using information in situated or critical ways. For example, Locke's (2009) study of education students showed that the graduate students who were interviewed associated information literacy with advancing new knowledge through research. Lupton (2008) conducted a study that compared tax law students and music students, finding that some tax law students' experiences of the relationship between information literacy and learning centered on preparing for their future professional lives, while some music students understood information literacy as being related to creating art through musical composition. Some students in these studies associated information literacy with personal change and growth (Locke, 2009; Lupton, 2004, 2008; Parker, 2006). A student in the study of education students summed up the link between information literacy and personal growth:

> Learning to use information effectively is an essential component of one's growth. Information and knowledge challenge where you stand and what you believe in and to be able to use information properly and appropriately and to be able to see the value of gathering information and gaining information it will change the way you are. Not necessarily who you are but what you think. (Student interview, Locke, 2009, p. 110)

In a study conducted by Lupton (2004), students in an environmental studies course had personal growth experiences, but some also focused on social change. These students experienced the relationship between information literacy and learning through a critical lens, carefully considering who was creating and providing the information they were encountering. These students focused on using what they learned to advocate for environmental change.

Bruce (2008) drew from the studies outlined above that reveal experiences of information literacy to create informed learning as a pedagogic strategy for enabling students to be able to use information with greater complexity. Informed learning is grounded in three principles (see Table 2.1). The teacher must design learning activities so that students learn about using information as well as about the topic

Table 2.1 Principles of informed learning

Principle	Description
1. Informed learning builds on learners' current informed learning experiences	Drawing from relational learning theory (Marton & Booth, 1997), teaching needs to acknowledge what students already know about what they are studying, and use that as a starting point for instruction intended to expand their awareness
2. Informed learning promotes simultaneous learning about disciplinary content and the information using process	Learning to use information and learning about disciplinary subject content are not separate, but instead are two parts of a whole. Therefore, a teacher would not provide one lesson on information skills, such as searching or evaluating, and then another lesson on understanding disciplinary concepts. Rather, students learn about disciplinary concepts, theories, and practices by engaging with information. The student may think of the disciplinary context and the ways they are expected to use information to be essentially the same. However, the teacher will be aware of both
3. Informed learning enables learners to experience using information and subject content in new ways	Informed learning must have a minimum of two goals. One goal will focus on the course content that learners are expected to know or be able to use. The other essential goal will focus on how students are intended to use information. Both should be part of the course assessment

Based on Bruce, C. S., & Hughes, H. (2010). Informed learning: A pedagogical construct for information literacy. *Library and Information Science Research*, 32(4), A2–A8.

of the course. By focusing on information literacy and content learning at the same time, learners come to experience using information within a context. For example, a master's course on cyber-learning aimed to have students understand and equip their practice as future educators in online environments (Hughes, 2012). To achieve this, the students learned to use online tools as they simultaneously learned about theories related to learning in online environments. Course learning goals typically focus on the topic but often include learning about disciplinary or professional practices, or, in some courses, applying a critical lens to explore a topic.

Outlined in Table 2.2, several characteristics also define informed learning (Bruce & Hughes, 2010). Teachers should consider the ways in which their students need to use information within a course, or in their future academic, personal, or professional lives, and design instruction that has students use information in those ways. In so doing, the students engage in disciplinary and vocational information

Table 2.2 Characteristics of informed learning

	Characteristics
Engaging with information	Awareness of different ways of using information Information practices drawn from disciplinary or professional practices Ethical uses of information
Subject content Information	Focuses on knowledge creation Disciplinary information Diverse forms of information, e.g., textual, visual, auditory, embodied, etc.
Pedagogy	Active learning techniques, such as collaborative and independent learning, problem-solving, evidence-based practice, and independent research Learners' previous experiences are drawn on Holistic approach to using information to learn Shared responsibility amongst educators in particular disciplines, information technologists, librarians, etc. Diverse student populations share perspectives
Transformative change	Learners may change their understandings of themselves, their discipline, and their professional practice

Based on Bruce, C. S., & Hughes, H. (2010). Informed learning: A pedagogical construct for information literacy. *Library and Information Science Research*, 32(4), A2–A8.

practices. Addressing Lloyd's (2010) point that information is not always textual, in an informed learning environment information is anything that is informing (Bruce, 2008). For example, in an environmental engineering course examining environmental issues in cities, information is regional demographic data, while in an art course, information is artistic works that provide inspiration for new work.

While it is not impossible to conceive of informed learning being conveyed through lecture, it usually involves active learning. For example, teachers might have their students work in teams to analyze and inform a problem, or they may have their students engage in practices of biologists to help students understand how biologists make decisions (Maybee, Doan, & Flierl, 2016). Recognizing how it will foster students' ability to use information in richer ways, informed learning aims to foster transformative experiences in which using information in new ways leads to personal or social change.

Informed learning is a flexible pedagogy that can be adopted in any learning environment if there are opportunities for using information. That is to say, informed learning, or at least aspects of it, can be used in tandem with other pedagogic strategies that are being adopted in higher education. For example, informed learning has been used to underpin an online module that also incorporated problem-based learning (Diekema, Holliday, & Leary, 2011). Hughes (2013) drew together ideas of inclusive approaches to learning with informed learning to offer a new model to address information literacy needs in culturally diverse higher education settings. Discussed in detail in Chapter 6, it has been combined with a motivational theory of learning to offer a model for developing motivating activities in which information is used to learn (Maybee & Flierl, 2017).

Informed learning would address many of the criticisms of the information skills approach to information literacy in higher education. By integrating information literacy into disciplinary courses, informed learning fosters students' abilities to use information within the varied educational contexts in which they are learning. Students' courses, taken across their college career, expose them to some different educational and social perspectives. Depending on a variety of contextual elements, including the topic and the teacher, different courses will aim to enculturate students into disciplinary or professional cultures. These courses provide opportunities for students to learn to use information as it is used within disciplinary or professional settings. Other courses will aim to make students aware of, and question, societal issues, norms, and values. The critical perspective of such courses provides opportunities for students to learn and reflect on the social influence and control that is exerted through the production and dissemination of information.

Adopting an informed learning approach to information literacy in higher education would provide students opportunities to practice using information in the contexts in which they are learning general education competencies, and in their majors when they are learning disciplinary or professional knowledge. Thus, an informed learning approach will better prepare students to use information in the practical ways necessary to be successful in their work and personal lives after college.

2.5 CONCLUSION

This chapter reviewed the literature on information literacy models in higher education. It highlighted the limitations of the information skills approach pervasive in higher education, and informed learning was put forward as an approach in which information literacy is an intrinsic part of the learning goals that underpin higher education course curricula. An informed learning approach would align with broader educational goals aimed at enculturating learners into disciplinary or professional roles, as well as provide them with a critical lens through which to challenge cultural and societal conventions. Implementing an informed learning approach in higher education would require academic librarians to partner more closely with teachers. Chapter 3 explores pathways for enabling academic librarians to engage in such partnerships.

REFERENCES

AACU. (2009). *Information literacy value rubric.* Retrieved fromAssociation of American Colleges and Universities. http://www.aacu.org/value/rubrics/information-literacy.

Accardi, M. T., Drabinski, E., & Kumbier, A. (Eds.), (2010). *Critical library instruction: Theories and methods.* Duluth, MN: Library Juice Press.

ACRL. (2000). *Information literacy competency standards for higher education.* Chicago, IL: Association of College and Research Libraries.

ACRL. (2008). Information literacy competency standards for anthropology and sociology students. Association of College and Research Libraries. Retrieved from http://www.ala.org/acrl/standards/anthro_soc_standards.

ACRL. (2011a). Information literacy competency standards for journalism students and professionals. Association of College and Research Libraries. Retrieved from http://www.ala.org/acrl/sites/ala.org.acrl/files/content/standards/il_journalism.pdf.

ACRL. (2011b). Information literacy competency standards for teacher education. Association of College and Research Libraries. Retrieved from http://www.ala.org/acrl/sites/ala.org.acrl/files/content/standards/ilstandards_te.pdf.

ACRL. (2013). Information literacy competency standards for nursing. Association of College and Research Libraries. Retrieved from http://www.ala.org/acrl/standards/nursing.

ACRL. (2015). Framework for information literacy for higher education. Association of College and Research Libraries. Retrieved from http://www.ala.org/acrl/standards/ilframework.

ALA. (1989). *Final report*. American Library Association. Retrieved from http://www.ala.org/ala/mgrps/divs/acrl/publications/whitepapers/presidential.cfm.

Andretta, S. (2012). *Ways of experiencing information literacy: Making the case for a relational approach*. Oxford: Chandos Publishing.

Barr, R. B., & Tagg, J. (1995). From teaching to learning: A new paradigm for undergraduate education. *Change, 27*(6), 12–25.

Bonner, A., & Lloyd, A. (2011). What information counts at the moment of practice? Information practices of renal nurses. *Journal of Advanced Nursing, 67*(6), 1213–1221. https://doi.org/10.1111/j.1365-2648.2011.05613.x.

Bonner, A., & Lloyd, A. (2012). Exploring the information practices of people with end-stage kidney disease. *Journal of Renal Care, 38*(3), 124–130. https://doi.org/10.1111/j.1755-6686.2012.00258.x.

Breivik, P. S., & Gee, E. G. (1989). *Information literacy: Revolution in the library*. New York: American Council on Education.

Brown, J. S., & Duguid, P. (2000). *The social life of information*. Boston: Harvard Business School Press.

Bruce, C. S. (1997). *The seven faces of information literacy*. Adelaide: Auslib Press.

Bruce, C. S. (2008). *Informed learning*. Chicago, IL: American Library Association.

Bruce, C. S., & Hughes, H. (2010). Informed learning: A pedagogical construct for information literacy. *Library and Information Science Research, 32*(4), A2–A8.

Bruce, C. S., Hughes, H., & Somerville, M. M. (2012). Supporting informed learners in the 21st century. *Library Trends, 61*(3), 522–545.

Bruce, C. S., Somerville, M. M., Stoodley, I., & Partridge, H. (2013). Diversifying information literacy research: An informed learning perspective. In M. Hepworth & G. Walton (Eds.), *Developing people's information capabilities: Fostering information literacy in educational, workplace and community contexts* (pp. 225–242). Bingley: Emerald Group Publishing Limited.

Bundy, A. (2004). Australian and New Zealand information literacy framework: Principles, standards and practice. Australian and New Zealand Institute for Information Literacy. Retrieved from http://www.anziil.org/resources/Info%20lit%202nd%20edition.pdf.

Cowan, S. M. (2014). Information literacy: The battle we won that we lost? *Portal: Libraries and the Academy, 14*(1), 23–32.

Diekema, A. R., Holliday, W., & Leary, H. (2011). Re-framing information literacy: Problem-based learning as informed learning. *Library & Information Science Research, 33*(4), 261–268.

Doyle, C. S. (1992). *Outcome Measures for Information Literacy within the National Education Goals of 1990. Final Report to National Forum on Information Literacy. Summary of Findings* [ERIC document No. ED 351033]. US Department of Education.

Drabinski, E., & Sitar, M. (2016). What standards do and what they don't. In N. Pagowsky & K. McElroy (Eds.), *1. Critical library pedagogy handbook*. Chicago: Association of College and Research Libraries.

Eisenberg, M., & Berkowitz, R. E. (1990). *Information problem-solving: The big six skills approach to library & information skills instruction*. Norwood, N.J: Ablex Pub. Corp.

Eisenberg, M., Lowe, C. A., & Spitzer, K. L. (2004). *Information literacy: Essential skills for the information age* (2nd ed.). Westport, Conn: Libraries Unlimited.

Elmborg, J. (2006). Critical information literacy: Implications for instructional practice. *Journal of Academic Librarianship, 32*(2), 192–199.

Freire, P. (1993). *Pedagogy of the oppressed (New rev 20th-Anniversary)*. New York: Continuum.

Giroux, H. A. (1988). *Teachers as intellectuals: Toward a critical pedagogy of learning*. Westport, CT: Bergin & Garvey.

Hofer, A. R., Brunetti, K., & Townsend, L. (2013). A thresholds concepts approach to the standards revisions. *Communications in Information Literacy, 7*(2), 108–113.

Hughes, H. (2012). Informed Cyber Learning: A case study. In P. Godwin & J. Parker (Eds.), *Information Literacy Beyond Library 2.0* (pp. 138–150). London: Facet Pub.

Hughes, H. (2013). International students using online information resources to learn: Complex experience and learning needs. *Journal of Further and Higher Education, 37*(1), 126–146.

Hughes, H., & Bruce, C. S. (2012). Snapshots of informed learning: LIS and beyond. *Education for Information, 29*, 253–269.

Irving, A. (1985). *Study and information skills across the curriculum*. London: Heinemann Educational Books.

Jackman, L. W., & Weiner, S. A. (2017). The rescinding of the ACRL 2000 Information Literacy Competency Standards for Higher Education—Really?? *College & Undergraduate Libraries, 24*(1), 117–119. https://doi.org/10.1080/10691316.2016.1217811.

Jacobson, T., & Mackey, T. P. (2011). Reframing information literacy as a metaliteracy. *College and Research Libraries, 72*(1), 62–78.

Kapitzke, C. (2003a). Information literacy: A positivist epistemology and a politics of outformation. *Educational Theory, 53*(1), 37–53.

Kapitzke, C. (2003b). Information literacy: A review and poststructural critique. *Australian Journal of Language and Literacy, 26*(1), 53–66.

Kerr, P. (2009). Espoused theories and theories-in-use of information literacy: A model for reflection and evaluation. *Proceedings of the American Society for Information Science and Technology, 46*(1), 1–7. https://doi.org/10.1002/meet.2009.1450460377.

Kuhlthau, C. C. (1993). *Seeking meaning: A process approach to library and information services*. Greenwich, CT: Ablex.

Lave, J. (1996). Teaching, as learning, in practice. *Mind, Culture & Activity, 3*(3), 149–164.

Lave, J., & Wenger, E. (1991). *Situated learning: Legitimate peripheral participation*. New York: Cambridge University Press.

Limberg, L. (1999). Experiencing information seeking and learning: A study of the interaction between two phenomena. Information Research, 5(1). Retrieved from http://informationr.net/ir/5-1/paper68.html.

Limberg, L. (2000). Is there a relationship between information seeking and learning outcomes? In C. S. Bruce, P. C. Candy, & H. Klaus (Eds.), *Information literacy around the world: Advances in programs and research.* Wagga Wagga, N.S.W: Charles Sturt University, Centre for Information Studies. [pp. 193–207].

Lloyd, A. (2007). Learning to put out the red stuff: Becoming information literate through discursive practice. *Library Quarterly,* 77(2), 181–198.

Lloyd, A. (2009). Informing practice: Information experiences of ambulance officers in training and on-road practice. *Journal of Documentation,* 65(3), 396–419.

Lloyd, A. (2010). *Information literacy landscapes: Information literacy in education, workplace and everyday contexts.* Oxford: Chandos.

Lloyd, A., Kennan, M. A., Thompson, K. M., & Qayyum, A. (2013). Connecting with new information landscapes: Information literacy practices of refugees. *Journal of Documentation,* 69(1), 121–144. https://doi.org/10.1108/00220411311295351.

Locke, R. A. (2009). *Learning information literacy: Qualitatively different ways education students learn to find and use information* [Masters Thesis]. Griffith University.

Lupton, M. (2004). *The learning connection: Information literacy and the student experience.* Adelaide: Auslib Press.

Lupton, M. (2008). *Information literacy and learning.* Blackwood, S. Aust.: Auslib Press.

Lupton, M., & Bruce, C. S. (2010). Windows on information literacy worlds: Generic, situated and transformative perspectives. In A. Lloyd & S. Talja (Eds.), *Practicing information literacy: Bringing theories of learning, practice and information literacy together* (pp. 4–27). Wagga Wagga, N.S.W.: Centre for Information Studies, Charles Sturt University.

Marton, F., & Booth, S. (1997). *Learning and awareness.* Mahwah, NJ: Lawrence Erlbaum.

Marton, F., Hounsell, D., & Entwistle, N. J. (1997). *The experience of learning: Implications for teaching and studying in higher education* (2nd ed.). Edinburgh: Scottish Academic Press.

Maybee, C. (2006). Undergraduate perceptions of information use: The basis for creating user-centered student information literacy instruction. *Journal of Academic Librarianship,* 32(1), 79–85.

Maybee, C. (2007). Understanding our student learners: A phenomenographic study revealing the ways that undergraduate women at Mills College understand using information. *Reference Services Review,* 35(3), 452–462.

Maybee, C., Doan, T., & Flierl, M. (2016). Information literacy in the active learning classroom. *Journal of Academic Librarianship,* 42(6), 705–711.

Maybee, C., & Flierl, M. (2017). Motivating learners through information literacy. In S. Kurbanoğlu, J. Boustany, S. Špiranec, E. Grassian, D. Mizrachi, L. Roy, & T. Çakmak (Eds.), Information Literacy in the Inclusive Society (Communications in Computer and Information Science Series): Proceedings of the 4th European Information Literacy Conference (pp. 698–707). Heidelberg: Springer.

Meyer, J. H. F., & Land, R. (2003). Threshold concepts and troublesome knowledge: Linkages to ways of thinking and practising within the disciplines. In C. Rust (Ed.), *Improving student learning theory and practice—10 years on* (pp. 412–424). Oxford: Oxford Centre for Staff and Learning Development.

MSCHE. (2003). Developing research & communication skills: Guidelines for information literacy in the curriculum. Middle States Commission on Higher Education. Retrieved from http://www.msche.org/publications/Developing-Skills080111151714.pdf.

MSCHE. (2009). Characteristics of excellence in higher education requirements of affiliation and standards for accreditation. Middle States Commission on Higher Education. Retrieved from http://www.msche.org/publications/CHX06_Aug08REVMarch09.pdf.

NEASC. (2005). Standards for accreditation.New England Association of Schools and Colleges Commission on Institutions of Higher Education Retrieved from http://cihe.neasc.org/downloads/Standards/Standards_for_Accreditation_2006.pdf.

Pappas, M., & Tepe, A. (2002). *Pathways to knowledge and inquiry learning.* Englewood, CO: Libraries Unlimited.

Parker, N. J. (2006). *Assignments, information and learning: The postgraduate student experience* [PhD Thesis]. Sydney: University of Technology, Faculty of Humanities and Social Sciences.

Pawley, C. (2003). Information literacy: A contradictory coupling. *The Library Quarterly, 73*(4), 422–452.

Reichel, M., & Arp, L. (1990). Library Literacy. *RQ, 30*(1), 46–49.

SCONUL. (2011). SCONUL seven pillars of information literacy: Core model for higher education. Society of College, National and University Libraries. Retrieved from http://www.sconul.ac.uk/topics_issues/info_literacy/.

Snavely, L., & Cooper, N. (1997). The information literacy debate. *The Journal of Academic Librarianship, 23*(1), 9–14. https://doi.org/10.1016/S0099-1333(97)90066-5.

Stripling, B. K., & Pitts, J. M. (1988). *Brainstorms and blueprints: Teaching library research as a thinking process.* Englwood, CO: Libraries Unlimited.

Tewell, E. (2015). A decade of critical information literacy: A review of the literature. *Communications in Information Literacy, 9*(1), 24–43.

Vikström, A. (2008). What is intended, what is realized, and what is learned? Teaching and learning biology in the primary school classroom. *Journal of Science Teacher Education, 19*(3), 211–233.

WASC. (2008). Handbook of accreditation 2008.Western Association of Schools and Colleges Retrieved from http://www.wascsenior.org/findit/files/forms/Handbook_of_Accreditation_2008_with_hyperlinks.pdf.

Webber, S., Boon, S., & Johnston, B. (2005). A comparison of UK academics' conceptions of information literacy in two disciplines: English and marketing. *Library and Information Research, 29*(93), 4–15.

Whitworth, A. (2014). *Radical information literacy: Reclaiming the political heart of the IL movement.* Burlington: Elsevier Science.

Zurkowski, P. G. (1974). *The information service environment relationships and priorities* [Related Paper No. 5]. National Commission on Libraries and Information Science, National Program for Library and, Information Services.

CHAPTER 3

Effecting Change Through Teaching and Learning Initiatives

Contents

Abstract

This chapter describes educational initiatives, such as service learning, undergraduate research, or faculty development programs, as providing opportunities for collaborations to integrate information literacy into higher education courses using an informed learning approach. Informed learning links using information directly to the learning of course content. Therefore, advancing this approach to information literacy requires academic librarians to collaborate with teachers and others who have oversight of, and can make changes to, courses. Teaching and learning initiatives provide access to higher education learning experiences, including the development of course curricula. The chapter concludes with a discussion of how to overcome challenges academic librarians may face in developing such collaborations.

Keywords: Educational initiatives, Collaboration, Faculty development, Course development, Information literacy integration, Informed learning.

3.1 INTRODUCTION

An informed learning approach to information literacy emphasizes having students learn to use information as they learn about disciplinary content (Bruce, 2008). Adopting an informed learning approach in higher education necessitates making changes to courses. From an informed learning perspective, integrating information literacy into a disciplinary course would likely involve revising course learning goals, activities, and assessments, so that they encompass both how students are expected to use information as well as what they are intended to learn about the course content. Without direct oversight of curricula, transiting to an informed learning approach in higher education could be challenging. For academic libraries to undertake such an enterprise requires that they be able to influence the development of course curricula.

To accomplish the integration of information literacy using an informed learning approach, it is imperative that academic librarians collaborate with teachers and others who have oversight and can make changes to courses. Teaching and learning initiatives provide access to higher education learning experiences, including the development of course curricula. Therefore, involvement in such initiatives offers promising opportunities for academic librarians aiming to partner with others to integrate informed learning into courses to allow students to learn to use, and practice using, information within a disciplinary learning context.

3.2 COLLABORATING FOR INFORMED LEARNING

Informed learning links using information directly to the learning of course content (Bruce, 2008). Integrating information literacy into courses using an informed learning approach would require academic librarians to collaborate with teachers. The academic library community has experience working to integrate information literacy into university curricula (Rockman, 2004a). Collaborations between teachers and librarians to integrate information literacy into curricula have been encouraged by academic library advocacy organizations, such as ACRL (2003a, 2003b). Examples abound in the scholarly literature of collaboration between academic librarians and teachers to integrate information literacy into higher education courses (Mounce, 2010).

However, most past collaborations to integrate information literacy are guided by the information skills approach espoused by ACRL's (2000) *Information Literacy Competency Standards for Higher*

Education. Applying the information skills approach to information literacy results in collaborations that focus on teaching students information skills as new content inserted into a disciplinary course. By not exploring how course content is learned through engagement with information, these efforts do not lead to informed learning. A brief examination of the two types of collaborative efforts will highlight the main differences between the two approaches. Identifying the differences will illuminate the elements academic librarians and their partners need to focus on when using an informed learning approach to integrate information literacy into courses.

Mounce's (2010) review of the scholarship examining librarian and teacher collaborations between 2000 and 2009 provides examples of collaborations that focus on developing students' information skills, and ones that focus on using information to learn about course content. A collaboration that focused on integrating information skills into a music survey course resulted in the librarian involved providing a library tour, teaching lessons on using the catalog music reference resources, citing sources according to *The Chicago Manual of Style*, and discussing copyright and intellectual property (Manus, 2009). These efforts are introducing a new content that is not directly related to the existing course content. Another example of an information skills approach had students in an introductory physics course conduct searches to supplement what they were learning in the course, such as gathering background information on scientists who developed laws or made discoveries discussed in class (Viele, 2006). In this case, the content students are learning to use is information related to physics, although it appears to be tangential to the main content of the course.

In contrast to the first two examples, another collaboration described in Mounce's (2010) review does connect learning course content with using information. In this collaboration, a teacher worked with librarians to design a genetics course in which students worked through literature-based scientific case studies aimed at introducing them to the process of scientific discovery (Elrod & Somerville, 2007). Predating the model developed by Bruce (2008), the design of the course was, in part, guided by the same ideas that lead to the creation of informed learning. In class, the students discussed case studies, working through questions about the researchers and the nature of their inquiry, data, and conclusions. Students formulated a genetics question of their own and searched for articles addressing it, as well as proposed a new experiment. Then the students were asked to select two papers cited in the references section of the original article and describe how those papers contributed to the experiment outlined in the original paper. As a culminating experience, students wrote their own literature-based scientific case study on a chosen topic in genetics. In this course, students were learning concepts related to the process of scientific discovery (course content) as they are also learning to find and analyze information (information literacy).

Adopting an informed learning approach requires that academic librarians analyze a learning context to determine how students should learn to use information as they engage with course content. Drawing from the characteristics of informed learning (Bruce & Hughes, 2010), the librarians need to identify what may be considered information, and how it may be used within a learning context. They may also need to determine or learn what types of information are used in the disciplinary or professional environments that are the focus of the course, how the information is used, and any ethical concerns surrounding its use. However, the main things to consider when working to integrate information literacy into a course using this approach are the three principles of informed learning:

(1)   Build on learners' current informed learning experiences.

(2)   Promote simultaneous learning about disciplinary content and the information use process.

(3)   Enable learners to experience using information and subject content in new ways (Bruce & Hughes, 2010).

From an informed learning perspective, there are two approaches an academic librarian can take when recommending that information literacy be integrated into a course. In the first approach, librarians identify how information is already being used, and determine if there are ways that they can improve how it is used to address information literacy goals better or enhance the learning of course content. The second approach that academic librarians may use to develop informed learning is to make recommendations for the inclusion of specific information literacy learning goals and activities not already included in a course, and then determine how they can be incorporated to support course content.

A librarian working with an engineering course offers an example of improving how information is used, or intended to be used, within a learning context. In this course, students interview their project partners to inform the needs and constraints of projects the students work on across the semester (Nelson, 2009). The librarian recognized that the students conducting the interviews were not always prepared or able to ask probing questions of the project partners. Thus, the students were incapable of gathering useful information to inform their project. As a result, the librarian added learning activities focused on crafting and conducting a quality interview. While not intentionally using an informed learning approach, this project does align with the three informed learning principles. Through prior experiences with the course, the librarian had recognized the students' experiences of conducting interviews. Building from that knowledge (principle 1), she developed the assignment to better inform the students' design efforts by learning to collect more thorough information (principle 2). Both the revised process of collecting the interview data and the information it provided presented a new way of approaching design work (principle 3).

The second approach, in which academic librarians make recommendations for the inclusion of specific information literacy learning goals and activities, would be the case if the collaborators decided that information literacy was an important learning outcome of the course that was not being addressed. Perhaps there is a mandate to include information literacy from an academic accrediting agency, or the course must meet a new college or university requirement. In such a case, the challenge would be for the collaborators to determine which information literacy concepts and practices they want to address. To generate discussion, a document that provides a broad overview of aspects of information literacy may be handy, such as ACRL's (2015) *Framework for Information Literacy for Higher Education*. As suggested by its creators, the *Framework* should not prescribe what information literacy concepts or practices to address. Instead, it can be used to generate possibilities, particularly if the teacher is unfamiliar with information literacy. The team would then need to decide how to integrate those concepts or practices in a way that students simultaneously learn both to use information and the content of the course.

3.3 INFLUENCING COLLEGE AND UNIVERSITY COURSES

With its emphasis on learning disciplinary content through using information, informed learning requires access to courses. One way of achieving this is for academic librarians to collaborate with teachers individually. While these are significant efforts, they do have the disadvantage of primarily drawing in teachers who already see the value in collaborating. As Wang (2011) was able to do with an engineering department, libraries that garner enough buy-in may be able to work at the departmental level to integrate information literacy, using an approach that links it to the learning context across an entire curriculum. However, for many academic libraries, the best way of reaching a wide array of courses is to partner with teaching and learning initiatives (Rockman, 2004b). Teaching and learning initiatives include first-year seminars and experiences, residential learning communities, writing across the curriculum, service learning, online learning, and faculty development programs. Some initiatives, such as undergraduate research, may provide co-curricular learning experiences that are outside of regular curricular offerings, but often these experiences are part of required or elective curricular offerings.

There are reasons that teaching and learning initiatives provide suitable venues for applying an informed learning approach to integrating information literacy into courses. For the most part, these initiatives are equally good places for using other methods for integrating information literacy as well. One reason for wanting to partner with teaching and learning initiatives is that they are usually associated with institutional agendas for improving teaching and learning (Iannuzzi, 1998). That is to say, the response to concerns about student retention may lead to the creation of a first-year or sophomore-year experience initiative to provide students with a stronger academic foundation, and more robust connections to the university community. Integrating information literacy into teaching and learning initiatives that support institutional goals may help ensure ongoing financial support. It also offers an opportunity to highlight the benefits of informed learning to the broader university community.

Perhaps the most important reason that teaching and learning initiatives are excellent venues for applying an informed learning approach is that they typically have a learning goal that can focus an academic librarian and a teacher's efforts to determine how students should use information in the course or other learning experience. That is, an initiative to develop student writing in upper-level undergraduate courses provides a context and goals for the librarian/ teacher collaboration, and efforts to draw information literacy into the project should revolve around identifying how students need to use information to learn about their topic and communicate their learning through writing. Similarly, applying an informed learning approach to integrating information literacy into a faculty development initiative to design online courses would focus on how learning in an online environment can be enhanced through specific kinds of engagement with information.

One of the ideas associated with informed learning is that educators may experience information literacy in various ways (Bruce, 1997, 2008). Different views of information literacy may be identified in teaching and learning initiatives as well. Riehle and Weiner (2013) reviewed the literature and reported that information literacy is a part of service learning, undergraduate research, writing-intensive courses, learning communities, and capstone experience initiatives. Using the ACRL (2000) *Standards* to frame the investigation, they identified various information skills students would likely learn when engaging in such experiences. For example, an undergraduate research experience involves many information skills, including gathering, organizing, interpreting primary and secondary sources, designing a research project, and communicating findings. If an academic librarian were using an informed learning approach when partnering with an undergraduate research initiative, he or she could help design activities in which students learned about and practiced these skills while engaged in their research.

In some instances, Riehle and Weiner (2013) reported that descriptions of information literacy in the articles they reviewed were related to the goals of a particular initiative. For example, one of the authors included in the review associated information literacy with the meaning-making that occurs within a learning community (Harris, 2008). Riehle and Weiner (2013) noted the transformative nature of experiences described by Eyler and Giles (1999) when describing how students adopted new perspectives that involved more complex approaches to using information when conducting investigations of issues related to their service learning work. If an academic librarian were applying an informed learning approach in partnering with either of these initiatives, the librarian would want to work with the teachers or staff to determine how using information could foster or extend these kinds of learning experiences.

Faculty development initiatives that focus on designing courses provide ample opportunity for integrating information literacy into college or university curricula using an informed learning approach. Typically these efforts concentrate on educational concerns, such as assessment, online learning, active learning, and so forth. In partnering with them, academic libraries work to integrate information literacy into the initiative in a way that aligns with and extends its goals. For example, academic librarians at Colgate University incorporated information literacy into a faculty development program in which information technologists and librarians worked with teachers to create media-based assignments, such as videos, blogs, and so forth. Example projects include a peace and conflict studies course assignment in which first-year students created podcasts about a world atrocity in which they needed to use information appropriately to communicate as an advocate, a journalist, or politician.

When there is enough institutional support, it is possible to have information literacy be the focus of a campus faculty development initiative. Such programs typically aim to inform teachers about information literacy and enable them to develop coursework that teaches students to use information. In fact, some believe it is necessary for disciplinary teachers to take responsibility for teaching students to use information and that academic libraries should create faculty development programs to support teachers in this endeavor (e.g., Cowan & Eva, 2017; Fister, 2009). The library at Earlham College provided an early, yet longstanding, example of working closely with teachers to integrate information literacy into curricula. Faculty development may take many forms, with some academic libraries offering grants to teachers to design information literacy-focused coursework. Others, such as the libraries at James Madison University, provide summer workshops in which teachers work with librarians to integrate information literacy into coursework.

Examples of larger scale faculty development programs that focused on integrating information literacy into curricula include a collaborative effort of a group of five liberal arts colleges in Ohio. The group, comprised of the College of Wooster, Denison University, Kenyon College, Oberlin College, and Ohio Wesleyan University, received Andrew W. Mellon Foundation funding for a project in which librarians partnered with teachers to develop information literacy-enriched course assignments and projects (Li, 2007). The librarians at Trinity University in San Antonio, Texas developed a 5-year quality-enhancement plan to integrate information literacy into curricula offered in each year of a students' college career (Millet, Donald, & Wilson, 2009). Supported by the institution's leadership, the program paired teachers with librarians to redesign an existing course or develop a new course.

It is easy to see how faculty development initiatives that primarily aim to integrate information literacy could apply an informed learning approach. The structure could take the form of one of the models outlined here, whether it be summer workshops or a more extensive program. Like these programs, each teacher participating would partner with an academic librarian. The chief difference would be in the description of information literacy and the activities through which it comes to be understood by the participants. Applying an informed learning approach, the librarian and teacher would work together to determine how students can learn to use information to enhance the learning of course content.

3.4 CHALLENGES TO INFORMED LEARNING COLLABORATIONS (AND HOW TO OVERCOME THEM)

Authors writing about collaborating and partnering with teaching and learning initiatives have identified some challenges to participating in these efforts. These challenges would also be likely to apply when working together to integrate information literacy using an informed learning approach. The first challenge is the perception that librarians are trying to "sell" information literacy, which can be an impediment to their being invited to participate in a teaching and learning initiative. Iannuzzi (1998) suggests that academic librarians pursuing involvement in teaching and learning initiatives must shift away from espousing the importance of information literacy. In line with an informed learning approach, Iannuzzi advises that librarians focus first on the mission of the initiative and consider how information literacy would further its goals. Focusing on the initiative's goals is important, for as she explains:

> ...the individuals who participate in these initiatives are as passionate, as consumed, as engrossed in their efforts as you are about the information literacy initiative.
>
> *(Iannuzzi, 1998)*

Building off Iannuzzi's (1998) point that the faculty and staff involved in creating and implementing teaching and learning initiatives have programmatic concerns of their own, they are also likely to be using educational theory to guide their efforts. Therefore, it is important to consider the interplay between informed learning and any other educational theories that underpin an initiative. In this regard, informed learning has proven to be a flexible pedagogy that works in tandem, or at least aspects of it can, with other ideas about teaching and learning adopted in higher education. For example, it has been used to underpin an online module that also incorporates problem-based learning (Diekema, Holliday, & Leary, 2011). Hughes (2013) drew together ideas of inclusive approaches to learning with informed learning to offer a new model to address information literacy needs in culturally diverse higher education settings.

A fundamental challenge to effective collaboration is that cultural differences between disciplinary teachers and academic librarians sometimes make it difficult for them to work together to integrate information literacy (Badke, 2005). While such differences may be hard to overcome, participating in a teaching and learning initiative may garner some buy-in for information literacy that might not be possible in another context. Teachers involved in such initiatives often receive a stipend for participation. They may also strongly believe in the goals of the initiative. Minimally, these external and internal motivators may ensure an openness to work taking place through the teaching and learning initiative.

Another challenge, however, is that teachers involved in collaborations to change a course sometimes feel that they are losing control of their curriculum. This concern may be even more prominent in an informed learning context where the goal is to change how content is learned. Fister (2009) cautions that it is important to recognize that teachers in higher education understand it is their responsibility to have students engage in inquiry. Therefore, they may feel ownership over concepts and practices that librarians consider to be part of information literacy (Weiner, 2014). Certainly, they will have implicit or explicit views of information literacy that align with their pedagogic perspective (Bruce, Edwards, & Lupton, 2006).

As suggested by Riehle and Weiner's (2013) review of the literature, information literacy may be construed differently depending on the goals for learning that underpin an initiative. For example, an initiative such as service learning may emphasize students' enculturation into disciplinary or professional practices, while a learning community focused on environmental concerns may want to foster transformative experiences in which students change their view of the world. In working with higher education teachers, it is essential to acknowledge their understandings and beliefs about information literacy even if they differ from one's own. Jumonville (2014), who was involved in the Trinity University project, suggests that it is important to make teachers feel that they have enough autonomy within the collaborative work of the initiative to determine how information literacy integrates into their courses.

Finally, in their project at Trinity University, Millet et al. (2009) recognized that the academic librarians working in their faculty development initiative needed professional development of their own to better support instructional design and educational technology. Academic librarians working today may have more experience with instructional design, however, they are unlikely to have experience applying design principles to develop goals, activities, and assessment for informed learning. It is likely academic librarians will learn to do so, as they have learned other new information literacy theories and practices that have emerged from research and made their way into practice. Applying an informed learning approach to integrate information literacy into college or university courses begins with reading about it in books such as this one, and then using the approach in one's instructional work, gaining experience over time.

3.5 CONCLUSION

This chapter discusses how academic librarians could advance an informed learning approach to information literacy through collaborations with higher education teachers. Teaching and learning initiatives are recommended as venues for such collaborations because they provide access to courses. Part 2 of this book provides an example of how an academic library may participate in a teaching and learning initiative by describing how Purdue Libraries partnered with other units on campus to create a faculty development program that aims to make foundational courses more student-centered. Purdue librarians work to integrate information literacy into the courses redesigned through this initiative. Beginning with Chapter 4, which provides an overview and background of the initiative, the six chapters that comprise Part 2 of this book examine different aspects of Purdue Libraries' efforts in creating and sustaining the initiative.

REFERENCES

ACRL. (2000). *Information literacy competency standards for higher education*. Chicago, IL: Association of College and Research Libraries.
ACRL. (2003a, revised 2012). Characteristics of programs of information literacy that illustrate best practices: A guideline. ACRL. Retrieved from http://www.ala.org/acrl/standards/characteristics.
ACRL. (2003b, June). Guidelines for instruction programs in academic libraries. ACRL. Retrieved from http://www.ala.org/acrl/standards/guidelines instruction.
ACRL. (2015). Framework for information literacy for higher education. Association of College and Research Libraries Retrieved from http://www.ala.org/acrl/standards/ilframework.
Badke, W. B. (2005). Can't get no respect: Helping faculty to understand the educational power of information literacy. *The Reference Librarian, 43*(89–90), 63–80. https://doi.org/10.1300/J120v43n89_05.
Bruce, C. S. (1997). *The seven faces of information literacy*. Adelaide: Auslib Press.
Bruce, C. S. (2008). *Informed Learning*. Chicago, IL: American Library Association.
Bruce, C. S., Edwards, S. L., & Lupton, M. (2006). Six frames for information literacy education: A conceptual framework for interpreting the relationships between theory and practice. *ITALICS (Innovations in Teaching and Learning Information and Computer Science), 51*(1), 1–18.
Bruce, C. S., & Hughes, H. (2010). Informed learning: A pedagogical construct for information literacy. *Library and Information Science Research, 32*(4), A2–A8.
Cowan, S., & Eva, N. (2017). Changing our aim: Infiltrating faculty with information literacy. *Communications in Information Literacy, 10*(2), 163–177.
Diekema, A. R., Holliday, W., & Leary, H. (2011). Re-framing information literacy: Problem-based learning as informed learning. *Library & Information Science Research, 33*(4), 261–268.

Elrod, S. L., & Somerville, M. M. (2007). Literature-based scientific learning: A collaboration model. *Journal of Academic Librarianship, 33*(6), 684–691. https://doi.org/10.1016/j.acalib.2007.09.007.

Eyler, J., & Giles, D. (1999). *Where's the learning in service-learning?* San Francisco: Jossey-Bass.

Fister, B. (2009). Fostering information literacy through faculty development. *Library Issues: Briefings for Faculty and Administrators, 29*(4).

Harris, B. R. (2008). Communities as necessity in information literacy development: Challenging the standards. *The Journal of Academic Librarianship, 34*(3), 248–255. https://doi.org/10.1016/j.acalib.2008.03.008.

Hughes, H. (2013). International students using online information resources to learn: Complex experience and learning needs. *Journal of Further and Higher Education, 37*(1), 126–146.

Iannuzzi, P. (1998). Faculty development and information literacy: Establishing campus partnerships. *Reference Services Review, 26*(3/4), 97–102.

Jumonville, A. (2014). The role of faculty autonomy in a course-integrated information literacy program. *Reference Services Review, 42*(4), 536–551.

Li, H. (2007). Information literacy and librarian-faculty collaboration: A model for success. Chinese Librarianship: An International Electronic Journal, 24. Retrieved from http://www.iclc.us/cliej/cl24li.pdf.

Manus, S. J. B. (2009). Librarian in the classroom: An embedded approach to music information literacy for first-year undergraduates. *Notes, 66*(2), 249–261. https://doi.org/10.1353/not.0.0259.

Millet, M. S., Donald, J., & Wilson, D. W. (2009). Information literacy across the curriculum: Expanding horizons. *College & Undergraduate Libraries, 16*(2–3), 180–193. https://doi.org/10.1080/10691310902976451.

Mounce, M. (2010). Working together: academic librarians and faculty collaborating to improve students' information literacy skills: A literature review 2000-2009. *Reference Librarian, 51*(4), 300–320.

Nelson, M. S. (2009). Teaching interview skills to undergraduate engineers: An emerging area of library instruction. Issues in Science and Technology Librarianship, 58. Retrieved from http://www.istl.org/09-summer/refereed3.html?a_aid=3598aabf.

Riehle, C. F., & Weiner, S. (2013). High-impact educational practices: An exploration of the role of information literacy. *College & Undergraduate Libraries, 20*(2), 127–143. https://doi.org/10.1080/10691316.2013.789658.

Rockman, I. F. (2004a). Integrating information literacy into the higher education curriculum: Practical models for transformation (1st ed.). San Francisco: Jossey-Bass. Retrieved from http://www.loc.gov/catdir/toc/ecip0412/2003027930.html; http://www.loc.gov/catdir/description/wiley041/2003027930.html.

Rockman, I. F. (2004b). Successful strategies for integrating information literacy into the currciulum. In *Integrating information literacy into the higher education curriculum: Practical models for transformation* (pp. 47–69). San Francisco: Jossey-Bass.

Viele, P. T. (2006). Physics 213: An example of faculty/librarian collaboration. *Issues in Science and Technology Librarianship, 47*.

Wang, L. (2011). An information literacy integration model and its application in higher education. *Reference Services Review, 39*(4), 703–720. https://doi.org/10.1108/00907321111186703.

Weiner, S. A. (2014). Who teaches information literacy competencies? Report of a study of faculty. *College Teaching, 62*(1), 5–12. https://doi.org/10.1080/87567555.2013.803949.

PART 2

Course Development at Purdue: A Case for Fostering Learning Through Information Literacy

CHAPTER 4

Purdue Libraries' Involvement in IMPACT

Contents

Abstract

This chapter provides an overview of a large-scale course redesign program created by the libraries in partnership with various other units at Purdue University. Called "Instruction Matters: Purdue Academic Course Transformation" (IMPACT), the program aims to enhance the success of Purdue students by making foundational courses more "student-centered," indicating a shift that places greater emphasis on fostering learning gains. Participants work in teams comprised of three teachers, an instructional developer, an educational technologist, and a librarian across 13 weekly meetings to revise various aspects of their course. The librarians involved in the IMPACT program strive to work with participants to integrate information literacy into courses in a way that supports content-focused learning.

Keywords: Course development, Course redesign, Educational initiatives, Faculty development, Student-centered learning

PROFILE: LIBRARIES ADMINISTRATOR

Tomalee Doan
Associate University Librarian for Engagement and Learning Services
Arizona State University

As head for Humanities, Social Science, and Business and later the Associate Dean for Faculty Affairs for Purdue University Libraries, I have had the fortune of being in the right place at the right time. Dr. Maybee writes about some of the ways in which I have been involved in Instruction Matters: Purdue Academic Course Transformation (IMPACT) in the chapter further. I am a true proponent of information literacy and student-centered learning. I became aware of the great value of student-centered learning when I concluded as a professional that today's student needs to be responsible for their learning and not do their coursework to get the grade. My experience in designing the first phase of an active learning classroom in the Roland G. Parrish Library in the Krannert School of Management, and my expertise in learning spaces and the student experience coupled with a high demand for instructional support librarians within the business curriculum led to my participation on the IMPACT Steering Committee. The IMPACT program, with its support from the Provost and President and its scale throughout the entire university, is like no other program in the country. Early on, the Provost's office recognized librarians as equal partners with the other six units involved in the program. Equally, the support of Library Dean James L. Mullins allowed me to participate in the IMPACT program, and his willingness to relinquish library space to create active learning classrooms as a prototype to learn about, do research, and collaborate with other campus units was crucial to the success of the program.

I felt it was important for the many subject librarians reporting to me to participate in IMPACT to demonstrate their skills and value, which would not only provide a different perspective but also serve our students and the Purdue instructional community. Purdue librarians have faculty status, and teaching and research as well as service are major components in their promotion and tenure process. Involving subject librarians proved to be a major success for both the Library and Purdue. Through their teaching, research, and service in IMPACT, librarians learned sound pedagogical practices and increased their confidence in contributing to the teaching excellence happening at Purdue, with the Library providing classroom library spaces that I designed. In turn, research conducted by the Office of Institutional Equity validated the effectiveness of the IMPACT program in student learning. As a result, the Indiana State Legislature provided $50 million for the new Thomas S. and Harvey D. Wilmeth Active Learning Center, which houses the Library of Engineering and Science and 27 class-rooms designed for active learning. This new center will enable both the valuable contributions of Purdue librarians and the IMPACT pro-gram to continue to grow and thrive at Purdue.

4.1 INTRODUCTION

In 2011, Purdue University undertook an initiative to redesign large, foundational courses, called "Instruction Matters: Purdue Academic Course Transformation" (IMPACT). The purpose of this endeavor was to enhance the success of Purdue students. To accomplish this goal, IMPACT aimed to make large, foundational courses "student-centered," which is an approach believed to have a positive influence on student learning. The idea at the heart of student-centered learning is that "learning" needs to be the focus of teaching activities (Barr & Tagg, 1995). While that may sound self-evident, proponents of student-centered learning argue that much teaching is "teacher-centered," meaning that it fulfils the teaching-related requirements, such as hold-ing class at regular intervals and exposing students to course content through lectures and reading. Student-centered approaches typically relinquish lecturing for more active learning activities that are more engaging for students. In a student-centered learning environment, students are encouraged to take ownership of their learning.

As outlined in Fig. 4.1, the IMPACT program has developed over time. It has changed in approach as well as grown in size, from ten teachers participating in the first cohort in 2011, to 50 participating each year since 2013. The university recently concluded an evalua-tion of the first 5 years of the IMPACT program (Purdue University, 2016). The program has had a significant impact on the campus, evi-denced by 68.2% ($n = 43,909$) of Purdue undergraduates having been registered for at least one course redesigned through the IMPACT

Fig. 4.1 Timeline of the IMPACT program

program since 2011. The ability to reach a large number of students is the result of 234 teachers redesigning 225 courses during the semester they participated in the IMPACT program, and redesigning an additional 113 courses on their own after completion of the formal training. Surveys of teachers who participated in the program have indicated that they are better able to articulate their goals for learning (89%, $n = 34$) and that the students are more active (69%, $n = 26$) and engaged (63%, $n = 24$) in the redesigned version of their course. Available data from student surveys reveal that 81.4% ($n = 18,534$) of these students rated the redesigned course they were taking as being highly student centered.

Purdue Libraries were one of the founding partners of the IMPACT program. In addition to being part of the group that envisioned it, the Libraries work with other organizations on campus to manage and implement the program. By engaging with teachers to develop student-centered learning through the program, librarians have also been able to find opportunities to integrate information literacy into course curricula. Describing Purdue Libraries' involvement in the IMPACT program, including why participation was in alignment with the Libraries' strategic goals, this chapter provides a brief history, outlining the impetus to establish the program and its development over time.

4.2 CREATION OF THE IMPACT PROGRAM

The IMPACT program was a response to a charge by Dale Whittaker, who at that time was the Vice Provost for Academic Affairs at Purdue. In 2010, Whittaker called together a group of administrators from various units on campus and asked them to develop a plan to foster student retention and success in large, foundational courses. A specific goal driving the program was to encourage student retention and lower what is referred to as the "DFW" rate. The DFW rate is the number of students who receive a grade of a D or an F, thus indicating substandard performance in a course, or withdraw from the course during the early part of the semester. Among the group that Whittaker called together was Tomalee Doan, then the Head of the Humanities, Social Sciences, and Business Division within the Purdue Libraries.

Doan was involved in the creation of various innovative learning spaces in the libraries that she oversaw. The first space designed by Doan was a 40-person learning lab with computers in the Parrish Library of Management and Economics (Doan & Kirkwood, 2011). Doan then recognized an emerging need for larger active learning classrooms on campus. While there were already active learning spaces at Purdue, they tended to seat thirty or fewer students. In response, Doan repurposed spaces in the Hicks Undergraduate Library. She began by creating an active learning classroom which opened in 2011 that would seat 117 students. The classroom arrangement was based on the "SCALE-UP" model, which was developed by a group at North Carolina State University (Beichner et al., 2007). The SCALE-UP model, which stands for "Student-Centered Active Learning Environment with Upside-down Pedagogies," has students work in groups of three, with three groups sitting at a round table. The creation of state-of-the-art learning spaces captured Whittaker's attention, and he invited Doan to join the original IMPACT development group.

The launch of the IMPACT program took place in 2011. The original mission of the program was "to improve student competency and confidence through the redesign of foundational courses by using research findings on sound student-centered teaching and learning" (IMPACT, 2011). Seven goals also guided these programmatic efforts:

- To refocus the campus culture on student-centered pedagogy and student success.
- To increase student engagement, competence, and learning gains.
- To develop a network of faculty, knowledgeable in teaching and learning best practices and passionate about teaching through Faculty Learning Communities (FLCs).
- To base course redesign on research-based pedagogies.
- To enhance and sustain IMPACT by adding new IMPACT participants annually.
- To support faculty-led course redesign with campus-wide resources.
- To reflect, assess, and share results to benefit future classes, students, and institutional culture (IMPACT, 2014).

Later replaced with an advisory group comprised of various stakeholders, a steering committee guided the development of the

IMPACT program during its first few years. A management team was also formed to create the program activities, conduct outreach activities, and manage the application and acceptance process. Doan served on both of these groups and was the sole representative from the Libraries until Clarence Maybee joined the Libraries as an information literacy specialist. Maybee joined Doan in serving on the management team, where they worked closely with their counterparts from Purdue's Center for Instructional Excellence (CIE) and the teaching and learning arm of Information Technology at Purdue (ITaP) to craft and shape the IMPACT program.

4.3 THE IMPACT PARTNERSHIP

The original units at Purdue involved in the creation of IMPACT have continued to participate, although in some cases unit names and staff may have changed due to reorganization efforts. See Fig. 4.2 for a graphic representing most of the original IMPACT partners, which notably places the teachers participating in the program, called "faculty fellows," at the center of IMPACT partnership. In addition to Purdue Libraries, partners include the President's Office, Office of the Provost, CIE, ITaP, the Evaluation & Learning Research Center (ELRC; this unit was formerly the Discovery Learning Research Center or

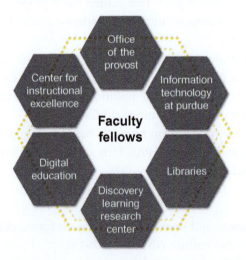

Fig. 4.2 Purdue units contributing to the IMPACT program (IMPACT partnership logo designed by Alejandra Carrillo-Munoz).

DLRC), Digital Education, and the Office of Institutional Research, Assessment and Effectiveness (OIRAE). The President's Office and the Office of the Provost provide funding for the IMPACT program. CIE, OIRAE, and the ELRC conduct assessment of the program. CIE collects and examines data related to student perceptions of student-centeredness and motivation in the courses redesigned through the program. The ELRC collects and analyzes data related to Purdue teachers' experiences of participating in the program. Originally, OIRAE examined aspects of student success, such as student grades and retention of students taking IMPACT courses. More recently, OIRAE has begun to oversee the evaluation of all three aspects of the assessment of IMPACT, by maintaining and analyzing the faculty and student perception data collected by CIE and the ELRC.

4.4 WHY THE LIBRARIES?

To some, it is surprising that Purdue Libraries are involved substantially in the creation of a university-wide course redesign program. Creating such a program does not align with academic library efforts focused on collection development, or even those efforts encompassed under the auspices of traditional information literacy programming. Three elements come together to create an environment in which Purdue Libraries saw the creation of the IMPACT program as an appropriate enterprise in which they should embark:

- Libraries' goals align closely with the University's goals for learning,
- visionary leadership that focused the Libraries' efforts on the vanguard of the University's efforts for learning, and
- Libraries faculty are flexible and nimble enough to be effective in a multifaceted, rapidly changing environment.

Led by James L. Mullins, Dean of Purdue Libraries, in recent years the Libraries worked to align their goals with the goals of the University. Information literacy is one of the Libraries' primary contributions to student learning on campus. A major goal of the Libraries' 5-year strategic plan introduced in 2011 was to make information literacy an integral part of undergraduate curricula and graduate programs (Purdue University Libraries, Press, and Copyright Office, 2016). Two objectives guided the Libraries towards the realization of this goal:

- Integrate information literacy into student learning at Purdue through partnerships and collaboration.
- Strengthen our capacity to lead and participate in information literacy and learning initiatives (Purdue University Libraries, Press, and Copyright Office, 2016).

During this period, Libraries' leadership wanted to reduce the number of one-time classroom visits by librarians, and increase information literacy efforts believed to be more impactful. The librarians were encouraged to work more closely and substantially with Purdue courses by providing multiple instruction sessions, co-teaching semester-long courses, or working with departmental faculty to embed information literacy assignments into coursework. The environment in the Libraries at Purdue supports innovation for projects that advance the Libraries' strategic goals. This support is evidenced by Doan being able to explore and create innovative spaces designed to promote student learning in the Libraries that she oversaw. Another aspect of the focus on innovation manifests in the Purdue Libraries' active search for opportunities to become involved with emerging campus teaching and learning initiatives, particularly ones that might enable the integration of information literacy into coursework.

4.5 THE IMPACT MODEL

Faculty and staff from CIE, ITaP, and Libraries facilitate the IMPACT program, which is grounded in a faculty learning community (FLC). An FLC is a model that brings together groups of teachers from across the university to actively engage in a curriculum focused on building community and taking scholarly approaches to enhancing teaching and learning (Cox, 2004). Each faculty fellow received $10,000 as an incentive for participation. The funds are to be used to improve the course being redesigned through the program.

The IMPACT program evolved. Although involved in the planning process, librarians were not members of IMPACT teams during the first iteration of the program. The program launch included 10 teachers in the summer of 2011. The teachers who participated were at varying stages of the redesign process. The group met in 3-hour sessions to discuss challenges they faced and brainstorm changes that they could implement to address those problems. In fall 2011, Purdue

Libraries faculty joined IMPACT teams for the second semester of the program. In the second iteration of the program, faculty and staff worked in teams of one teacher, a librarian, and a staff person from CIE and ITaP. If necessary, the same staff and faculty work with the teachers after the semester they participate in the IMPACT program to continue to enhance the course.

In 2013, the IMPACT program adopted its current model. In January of 2013, Mitch Daniels became the twelfth President of Purdue University after serving his second term as Governor of the State of Indiana. Daniels founded "Purdue Moves," which is a series of initiatives intended to address challenges facing higher education. The four areas dealt with by Purdue Moves are affordability and accessibility, STEM leadership, world-changing research, and transformative education. The IMPACT program is one of the initiatives aimed at fostering transformative education. At this time, the program received additional funding along with the request that the program expand its efforts to redesign courses in Purdue's core curriculum, and that the program increase in size. Up to this point, the program had been working with ~30 teachers each year, whereas now the expectation was to work with 60 teachers a year. The IMPACT model was changed to accommodate the increase in participation, resulting in three teachers on teams with a librarian, and staff from CIE and ITaP.

A primary focus of the IMPACT program early on was enabling teachers to select a model that would provide a structure they could use to frame the course. The teachers participating in the program were introduced to course design models, such as replacement, supplemental, emporium, and so forth, mostly drawn from the National Center for Academic Transformation (NCAT) (Twigg, 2003). Teachers were also introduced to problem-based, case-based, and inquiry-guided learning models. In 2013, a new director of the Center for Instructional Excellence drew from her psychology background to refocus the IMPACT FLC curriculum to emphasize student motivation. This resulted in a shift that deemphasized course design models. The program came to be grounded in a motivational theory called self-determination theory (Ryan & Deci, 2000), which placed greater importance on student perceptions of their competence and autonomy in a course as well as how connected students feel to their teacher and other students.

4.6 DAY-TO-DAY IN IMPACT

As outlined in Table 4.1, the thirteen 75-min weekly FLC meetings are structured so that the topics discussed align with the stages of backward design (Wiggins & McTighe, 2005). Backward design is an instructional design model that emphasizes the need to first identify learning goals before determining other elements of course design, such assessment instruments, and learning activities.

After the first meeting introducing the program, the next three weeks of the FLC curriculum are dedicated to teachers learning about a framework for student motivation and creating learning outcome statements that reflect their intentions for student learning in the course. While some teachers, particularly in departments strongly influenced by standards from an accrediting body, have previously prepared learning outcomes, for many developing such statements is

Table 4.1 Weekly topics and deliverables of IMPACT FLC meetings

Session	Topic	Major deliverables
Session 1	Kick-off	
Session 2	Teaching goals and student characteristics	Initial learning outcomes
Session 3	Motivation and cognition theories of learning	Initial redesign goal
Session 4	Learning outcomes and objectives	
Session 5	Assess student performance, part 1	Revised learning outcomes
Session 6	Assess student performance, part 2	Learning objectives
Session 7	Learning activities, part 1	
Session 8	Learning activities, part 2	Initial assessment map
Session 9	Connecting the dots	
Session 10	Redesign decisions	Revised redesign goal
Session 11	Redesign presentations	Revised assessment map (including revised redesign goal and revised learning objectives)
Session 12	Scholarly and reflective practitioner	
Session 13	Closing the loop and focus group	Evidence of learning data plan

a new activity. The teachers also identify learning objectives, which the program defines as lesson-level goals for learning that collectively enable students to achieve a course-level learning outcome.

The fifth and sixth weeks focus on teachers determining how they may know if their students are meeting the newly crafted learning outcomes and objectives. A major part of this work is aligning assignment instruments to outcomes and objectives. Beginning with the seventh week, the focus shifts to the teachers identifying learning activities intended to motivate students to learn and prepare them to complete the course assessments. It is here that the teachers are asked to consider how the students need to use information to succeed in the course. In the remaining weeks, teachers report out across teams about the choices they have made, and indicate how the changes will motivate their students and make the course more student-centered.

The teachers who are participating in the program complete "deliverables" that reflect their progress through the IMPACT course redesign process. During the first week, the teachers are asked to articulate a "goal for their redesign" to guide their redesign work. The learning outcomes and objectives for the course, developed iteratively during the first few weeks of the semester, are also collected. The teachers create an assessment plan in which they map their final exam or class project to their learning outcomes and objectives. In completing this task, the teachers often come to recognize the need for changes to an exam or another assessment instrument to allow it to properly inform them of students' progress towards meeting a select learning outcome or objective.

Much of the redesign work occurs in the discussions that take place both at the weekly meetings or in team meetings scheduled by the team leader. While the librarians and staff from CIE and ITaP collectively work with the teachers to develop student-centered learning, each team member also shares their expertise. CIE supports the application of innovative pedagogies, ITAP assists with the adoption of educational technologies, and the librarians collaborate with teachers to integrate information literacy into the coursework. The rest of the chapters that comprise Part 2 of this book (Chapters 5 through 9) will describe the librarians' efforts in working with teachers participating in the IMPACT program to integrate information literacy into undergraduate courses at Purdue.

4.7 CONCLUSION

In partnering on the creation and implementation of the IMPACT program, Purdue Libraries showed initiative to campus leaders, indicating to them that the Libraries recognized that their mission involves advancing student learning. Through the IMPACT program, the Libraries have been able to achieve strategic goals of partnering to integrate information literacy into course curricula. The current chapter provides an overview of the Purdue Libraries' role in creating and sustaining the IMPACT program. Chapter 5 shifts from outlining general aspects of the IMPACT program to describe the efforts of Purdue librarians on IMPACT teams. As team members, librarians participating in the IMPACT program adopt a coaching model to working with teachers to redesign Purdue courses, both to make the courses more student-centered and, when possible, to integrate information literacy.

REFERENCES

Barr, R. B., & Tagg, J. (1995). From teaching to learning: A new paradigm for undergraduate education. *Change, 27*(6), 12–25.
Beichner, R. J., Saul, J. M., Abbott, D. S., Morse, J. J., Deardorff, D. L., Allain, R. J., et al. (2007). The student-centered activities for large enrollment undergraduate programs (SCALE-UP) project. In E. F. Redish & P. J. Cooney (Eds.), Research-based reform of University physics (pp. 3–10).
Cox, M. D. (2004). Introduction to faculty learning communities. *New Directions for Teaching and Learning, 2004*(97), 5–23. https://doi.org/10.1002/tl.129.
Doan, T., & Kirkwood, H. (2011). Strategically leveraging learning space to create partnership opportunities. *College & Undergraduate Libraries, 18*(2–3), 239–248. https://doi.org/10.1080/10691316.2011.577692.
IMPACT. (2011, December,). IMPACT Mission Statement. Retrieved from http://www.purdue.edu/impact. (Accessed 16 April 2017).
IMPACT. (2014). IMPACT annual report. West Lafayette: Purdue University. Retrieved from https://www.purdue.edu/impact/assets/documents/IMPACT%20annual%20report%202014(I).pdf.
Purdue University. (2016). *IMPACT: Instruction Matters: Purdue Academic Course Transformation (Institutional Report).* West Lafayette, IN: Purdue University. Retrieved from https://www.purdue.edu/impact/assets/documents/IMPACT%20annual%20report%202016.pdf.
Purdue University Libraries, Press, and Copyright Office. (2016). Strategic plan 2011–2016: The faculty of library, archival and information sciences. Retrieved from https://www.lib.purdue.edu/sites/default/files/admin/plan2016.pdf.

Ryan, R. M., & Deci, E. L. (2000). Intrinsic and extrinsic motivations: Classic definitions and new directions. *Contemporary Educational Psychology, 25*(1), 54–67. https://doi.org/10.1006/ceps.1999.1020.

Twigg, C. (2003). Improving learning and reducing costs: New models for online learning. *EDUCAUSE Review, 38*(5), 28–38.

Wiggins, G. P., & McTighe, J. (2005). *Understanding by design* (2nd ed.). Alexandria, VA: Association for Supervision and Curriculum Development.

CHAPTER 5

Librarians as Coaches

Contents

Abstract

This chapter discusses the coaching role that librarians involved in the IMPACT program adopt in their work with teachers to redesign courses. These librarians must be knowledgeable of innovative teaching and learning practices, able to build relationships across departments or other boundaries, and able to develop shared goals with their partners. When working with teachers participating in IMPACT, librarians look for opportunities to show how information literacy may support the creation of student-centered learning environments. The backward design instructional model, which prompts designers to focus separately on creating learning outcomes, assessments, and learning activities, provides a structure through which librarians can discuss aspects of information literacy in relation to a teacher's goals for learning.

Keywords: Librarians as coaches, Librarians as consultants, Backward design, Librarian and teacher collaboration, Academic librarians.

PROFILE: IMPACT TEAM MEMBER

Catherine Fraser Riehle

Learning Resources Design Librarian
University of Nebraska, Lincoln

In my former role as a faculty librarian at Purdue University Libraries, I had the pleasure of serving as a consultant and support team member for over twenty Instruction Matters: Purdue Academic

Course Transformation (IMPACT) teachers on course redesign projects. For these projects, teachers' goals ranged from scaling up a course for a new program to integrating more active learning opportunities throughout a semester. The experience provided me a wider and valuable community of practice related to teaching and learning, which honed and shaped my practice and professional identity.

Participating in IMPACT includes membership in a community of librarians, instructional developers, educational technologists, and teachers from a variety of disciplines. Members of each group bring a variety of perspectives. The blending of complementary sets of expertise in the redesign process positively influenced teachers' redesigns while expanding our toolkits, as consultants, in areas related to teaching and learning. Because of my involvement in IMPACT, my network for referrals and teaching and learning-related projects grew considerably wider. Within a semester or two of being involved in IMPACT, if I or someone I encountered had a question or problem related to teaching and learning, I almost certainly knew someone who could answer or help solve it.

IMPACT provided me the opportunity to collaborate with colleagues with whom I had not worked previously. In some of my liaison areas, it opened previously closed or difficult-to-open doors to conversations about teaching and learning and information literacy in curricula, as participation in the program shifted the context of those conversations. In the context of course redesign, I was not a "service provider" seeking to integrate information literacy into a course or curriculum, but instead, a consultant and collaborator, participating in conversations about (often shared, it turned out) learning goals and outcomes. This subtle but significant shift, I believe, made all the difference for developing trust and meaningful collaboration. Now I borrow from the backward design framework when I talk with teachers about teaching and learning in general or information literacy in particular. Instead of asking, "What tools, resources, or instruction might your students need?" I ask, "With what do your students struggle?" and "What do you want your students to understand or be able to do?"

In my role as an IMPACT consultant, I strove to be an active listener—I served as a sounding board, brainstorming partner, and provider of constructive criticism—and I asked a lot of questions. While my role involved a significant amount of listening (e.g., in response to, "Tell me the most important thing you want your students to get out of this class") and question-asking (e.g., "How should students be able to demonstrate they understand that?"), I noticed my voice became clearer every semester. With experience and increased knowledge of learning theory and pedagogical best practices, my confidence as a consultant grew, my professional identity made room for these new roles, and my conceptualization of information literacy became stronger and something I could more easily articulate in a variety of disciplinary contexts, instructor challenges, course goals, and learning outcomes.

5.1 INTRODUCTION

Working closely with the teachers across the semester-long IMPACT program, the librarians try to accomplish two things. First, they work to make foundational courses at Purdue more student-centered. Making Purdue courses student-centered is the primary mission of the IMPACT program and a shared goal of the librarians, the instructional developers in CIE, the instructional technologists in ITaP, and the teachers. Second, the librarians want the teachers with whom they work to see the value of information literacy and to integrate it into their courses. While learning about information literacy may be an appropriate development goal for Purdue teachers, particularly those teaching foundational courses, it is, nonetheless, not a formal goal of the IMPACT program. It is left to Purdue librarians to introduce the teachers to information literacy and get them to consider how their approach to having their students use information to complete coursework may influence what they learn.

The coaching role that librarians participating in the IMPACT program adopt in their work with teachers requires that they be knowledgeable regarding innovative teaching and learning practices, and able to build relationships and develop shared goals with their partners. The librarians working with IMPACT have become very knowledgeable of teaching and learning theories and models that support the development of student-centered learning environments. They have been extremely successful at building relationships and developing shared goals to guide the work they do with teachers and faculty and staff from the other units involved in IMPACT. Librarians look for opportunities to show how information literacy may support the creation of student-centered learning environments. The conversations in which librarians introduce different ways of using information to foster student-centered learning occur over time during the IMPACT weekly FLC sessions and additional team meetings. The backward design model introduced by Wiggins and McTighe (2005), which prompts designers to focus separately on creating learning outcomes, assessments, and learning activities, provides a structure through which librarians can discuss aspects of information literacy in relation to a teacher's goals for learning.

5.2 CHARACTERISTICS OF QUALITY COACHING

Purdue librarians view their role on IMPACT teams as "coaches" to the teachers whose courses are redesigned through the program (Flierl, Maybee, Riehle, & Johnson, 2016). Although the librarians recognized that they were coaching the teachers involved in the IMPACT program, they were not using a particular coaching model in their work. Michael Flierl, then the Purdue Libraries' Information Literacy Instructional Designer, decided to examine the scholarly literature to determine how coaching models compared to the efforts of the Purdue librarians. The result of his review is included in a book chapter written by Purdue librarians about their experiences of integrating information literacy through their efforts in the IMPACT program (Flierl et al., 2016). The approach taken by librarians working with IMPACT shared characteristics with "information consulting" models (Frank & Howell, 2003; Frank, Raschke, Wood, & Yang, 2001; Vickers, 1992). Flierl noted three main aspects of consulting models as important to the work academic librarians engage in when coaching:

- knowledge and abilities,
- relationship building, and
- developing and accomplishing goals (Flierl et al., 2016).

The knowledge and abilities needed by a consultant include being able to contribute to a team and cultivate institutional support (Frank & Howell, 2003; Frank et al., 2001; Vickers, 1992). Relationship building involves being able to integrate into a scholarly community and engage with scholars as equal partners. Finally, developing and accomplishing goals includes sharing solutions around a client's, namely teachers, actual needs and promoting a variety of solutions. These are different from traditional liaison skills, and highlight the shifting roles of librarians as they engage with information literacy and student learning in collaboration with partners outside of the library.

The librarians who began working with IMPACT in 2012 had already learned innovative ideas about teaching and learning to improve the information literacy instruction they provided to courses in their liaison areas. When they joined IMPACT, they collectively possessed knowledge of various approaches to active learning through their explorations and experiences using these methods in their teaching. While librarians were more knowledgeable of ideas about student-centered learning than many of the teachers, in the early days they learned a tremendous amount from their colleagues on the teams who were instructional developers and technologists from CIE and ITaP. They were mostly familiar with approaches widely used at Purdue, such as problem-based learning in which students typically work in teams through a process to develop a solution to a complex problem. The first few months of their involvement in IMPACT, the group of librarians involved met regularly to share their knowledge with each other. The ideas explored in the weekly meetings were another way that librarians expanded their knowledge of teaching and learning. Over time, the knowledge about teaching and learning of the librarians involved in the IMPACT project has increased tremendously.

The IMPACT program itself is a form of institutional support for student-centered learning. The arrangement of a librarian, an instructional developer, and a technologist working with the teachers was a strategy to expose teachers to particular kinds of institutional support available to them. The knowledge required of the librarians who work on IMPACT teams is a broad understanding of how to create a student-centered learning environment. Creating this kind of environment involves several elements, such as using active learning pedagogic approaches, and teaching and assessing in ways that encourage motivation in students. A student-centered learning environment may also include information literacy. As the teachers and others working on IMPACT teams may have varying views, it is beneficial for librarians on the team to be familiar with a wide array of information literacy theories and models.

As liaisons to specific departments, librarians are familiar with strategies for building relationships. Therefore, the librarians were well placed from the beginning of their time in IMPACT to make headway with this aspect of the work. Exemplifying this, a librarian working with the IMPACT program describes the continuing involvement she is having with a technology course that was redesigned through the IMPACT program in 2012:

> *A distinguishing characteristic of this course is the ability of the embedded librarian to participate as an equal partner in the instructional process. The instructional team of the course consists of each instructor of every course section, course graders, and graduate students. I have been a part of the weekly instructional team meetings, contributing to the detailed conversations about the course and the assignments, as any other member of the team. These interactions have strengthened the relationships of the library and course coordinators, while also providing opportunities for refined iterations of the MIL [media and information literacy] instructional content over time and practice (IMPACT Librarian Reflection 2, in Flierl et al., 2016).*

The last element of coaching described by Flierl and his colleagues (2016) was developing and accomplishing goals. Here they note that coaching the teachers in IMPACT needs to be collaborative, rather than cooperative, in nature. Collaboration suggests that both parties are partnering to accomplish a shared goal, rather than cooperating in a way that each party reaches their own separate goal (Frank et al., 2001). As mentioned previously, the shared goals amongst the teachers, CIE and ITaP faculty and staff, and the librarian on each team is to create a student-centered learning environment. Information literacy is only relevant if it is critical to the creation of such an environment. As they work with the team to redesign a course, the librarians are also looking for ways that information literacy may support the student-centered learning environment being developed by the group.

5.3 THE COMMON GROUND OF INSTRUCTIONAL DESIGN

Instructional design models, sometimes referred to as curriculum design, can provide a common focus for discussing elements of instruction. The IMPACT curriculum that the faculty learning community (FLC) goes through is grounded in backward design (Wiggins & McTighe, 2005). It is called "backward" because, unlike other design models that begin by selecting things such as technology or learning space, the design process starts with determining the goals for learning. The design model is grounded in constructivist learning theory (Vygotsky and Cole 1978), and as such sees teaching as a way to enable deeper understandings, rather than memorization. Specifically developed for use in education, backward design focuses on enhancing student learning, rather than emphasizing what will be taught. As previously stated, backward design is comprised of three stages, in which teachers develop: (1) learning outcomes that describe what students will know or be able to do after the course, (2) assessment that shows if students can perform as intended, and (3) learning activities that enable students to achieve the learning outcomes and perform as desired (Wiggins & McTighe, 2005). In IMPACT, several FLC meetings focus on the three stages of backward design.

When each of the three stages of the backward design process (Wiggins & McTighe, 2005) is the focus of an FLC session, librarians and the others on the IMPACT team work with the teachers to reconsider the learning outcomes, assessment, and learning activities for the course they are redesigning through the program. The process may also provide opportunities to discuss information literacy with the teachers. Early on in their participation in the IMPACT program, the teachers share the learning outcomes they were using for their course before joining the program. The teachers are given feedback from their team to consider as they work to revise the learning outcomes. When appropriate, the librarians encourage the teachers to consider if students need to learn to use information to be successful in the course, and if so, how that should be reflected in the learning outcomes.

IMPACT teams also discuss different types of assessment. They consider the need for formative assessment techniques that provide students the opportunity to get feedback to improve their performance, and summative assessment methods that measure students' performance at the end of the course or sequence. If information literacy is reflected in the learning outcomes, the librarians on the team encourage the teachers to consider how it should be assessed in the course. The teacher works with the team members to create an assessment plan that links their assessment to their learning outcomes. After determining assessment, the teams brainstorm learning activities that will enable students to achieve the learning outcomes for the course.

Frequently the activities the group brainstorms require the students to engage with information, providing an opportunity for the librarians working with the teachers to integrate information literacy into the course in a way that supports learning gains.

Backward design provides the librarians and faculty and staff from CIE and ITaP a process by which to work with the teachers participating in the IMPACT program. The process aims to ensure that attention is focused on three key aspects of the course being redesigned: learning outcomes, assessment, and learning activities. Focusing on the three stages of backward design in the FLC meetings also provides a shared timeline and understanding of goals for the librarians and the faculty and staff from CIE and ITaP to coordinate their coaching efforts. In addition to supporting the librarians in their work in the IMPACT program, backward design also supports them in their teaching, and collaborations they have with teachers or others working to create learning environments outside of the IMPACT program.

5.4 A SHARED LANGUAGE OF LEARNING

There is not widespread agreement about the nature of information literacy. The boundaries of it have been explored by comparing information literacy to related concepts, such as media literacy or digital literacy (Bawden, 2001). As described in the ACRL *Framework* (2015), Jacobson and Mackey (2011) suggest that information literacy is an overarching concept that encompasses media, digital, and other literacies. The different descriptions of information literacy are associated with an epistemological stance that aligns with a social or educational theory (Limberg, Sundin, & Talja, 2012). That is to say, someone with a socio-culturalist perspective would likely view information literacy as adopting information practices, while someone with a critical theory perspective may focus on the role information plays in determining social capital. The illusiveness of the concept can make it difficult for librarians to explain information literacy to others. Complicating matters even further, teachers that librarians work with will have their own understanding, explicit or implicit, of information literacy, which is likely to be associated with their views of teaching and learning (Bruce, Edwards, & Lupton, 2006). The librarians working in

IMPACT regularly navigate the varied points-of-view around information literacy when working with the teachers.

Drawing from his experiences on IMPACT teams, Michael Flierl (2017) has written about how librarians should approach discussing information literacy with teachers in other disciplines. Using the concept of "language games" described by Wittgenstein (2009), Flierl points out how people use the same terms to mean different things. Flierl suggests that when librarians discuss information literacy they are considering "innumerable factors such as ethical, pedagogical, and even political elements, amongst others" of which teachers from other disciplines are unlikely to be aware. Specific words may have different meanings for teachers and librarians. To avoid misunderstandings, Flierl offers three questions that librarians may use to discuss information literacy with teachers:

1. What do you want students to know, do, or value as a result of your class?
2. How do students use or engage with information in your class to accomplish learning goals?
3. Should student engagement with information be distinct from or integrated with course content? (Flierl, 2017)

Flierl (2017) explains that the first question purposefully does not focus on information or information literacy. Instead, this question aids the librarian to understand the teacher's intentions for learning. Once learning goals are established, the second question then focuses in on how using information fosters or supports intended learning in the course. The answer to the first question provides important context for understanding the answer to the second question. The purpose of the third question is to determine if the teacher perceives a close relationship between using information and course content within the class. If the teacher views using information as interrelated with learning course content, the librarians can use their expertise to suggest how more frequent or different types of engagement with information may encourage greater student learning.

Flierl's (2017) description of librarians working with teachers to integrate information literacy into coursework is similar to how other librarians involved in IMPACT have described their experiences coaching teachers. By connecting information literacy directly to student learning, librarians can reach the goal of creating student-centered learning environments as well as advancing information literacy at Purdue. Rather than being another educational idea promoted by the Purdue Libraries or the University, information literacy becomes relevant to teachers when it is seen as supporting learning in a student-centered learning environment.

5.5 CONCLUSION

This chapter discussed approaches and strategies taken by librarians involved in the IMPACT program to support the development of student-centered learning environments at Purdue. Working with teachers and others involved in the IMPACT program, the librarians focus on program goals and look for opportunities to discuss how information literacy may support the development of student-centered learning environments. Chapter 6 discusses how librarians working with the IMPACT program have engaged with the educational theories and models used in the IMPACT program, and have been able to draw them together with the informed learning approach to information literacy to develop new educational tools.

REFERENCES

ACRL. (2015). *Framework for information literacy for higher education*. Association of College and Research Libraries. Retrieved from http://www.ala.org/acrl/standards/ilframework.

Bawden, D. (2001). Information and digital literacies: A review of concepts. *Progress in Documentation, 57*(2), 218–259.

Bruce, C. S., Edwards, S. L., & Lupton, M. (2006). Six frames for information literacy education: A conceptual framework for interpreting the relationships between theory and practice. *ITALICS (Innovations in Teaching and Learning Information and Computer Science), 51*(1), 1–18.

Flierl, M. (2017). *Information literacy dialogue as a Wittgensteinian language game: Embedding IL into curricula*. In S. Kurbanoğlu, J. Boustany, S. Špiranec, E. Grassian, D. Mizrachi, L. Roy, & T. Çakmak (Eds.), *Information literacy in the inclusive society (communications in computer and information science series): Proceedings of the 4th European information literacy conference*. (pp. 688–687). Heidelberg: Springer.

Flierl, M., Maybee, C., Riehle, C. F., & Johnson, N. (2016). IMPACT lessons: Strategically embedding MIL through teacher development in higher education. In D. Oberg & S. Ingvaldsen (Eds.), *Media and Information literacy in higher education: Educating the educators* (pp. 119–133). Oxford: Chandos.

Frank, D., & Howell, E. (2003). New relationships in academe: Opportunities for vitality and relevance. *College and Research Libraries News, 64*(1), 24–27.

Frank, D., Raschke, G., Wood, J., & Yang, J. (2001). Information consulting: The key to success in academic libraries. *Journal of Academic Librarianship, 27*(1), 90–96.

Jacobson, T., & Mackey, T. P. (2011). Reframing information literacy as a metaliteracy. *College and Research Libraries, 72*(1), 62–78.

Limberg, L., Sundin, O., & Talja, S. (2012). Three theoretical perspectives on information literacy. *Human IT, 11*(2), 93–130.

Vickers, P. (1992). Information consultancy in the UK. *Journal of Information Science, 18,* 259–267.

Vygotsky, L. S., & Cole, M. (1978). *Mind in society: The development of higher psychological processes.* Cambridge: Harvard University Press.

Wiggins, G. P., & McTighe, J. (2005). *Understanding by design* (2nd ed.). Alexandria, VA: Association for Supervision and Curriculum Development.

Wittgenstein, L. (2009). In P. M. S. Hacker & J. Schulte (Eds.), *Philosophische Untersuchungen (English).* Malden: Wiley. G. E. M. Anscombe, Trans.

CHAPTER 6

Higher Education Teachers' Views of Information Literacy

Contents

Abstract

This chapter provides a brief overview of the research into classroom teachers' views of information literacy, and outlines the findings of a research team at Purdue that investigated how teachers who had completed the IMPACT program addressed information literacy in their active learning courses. The findings revealed three major themes focused on: (1) students learning information or technology skills, (2) students engaging in information-related activities that lead directly to learning subject content, and (3) students understanding and applying disciplinary information practices. Academic librarians can use these findings to determine how teachers with whom they are collaborating understand information literacy, which may aid them in developing shared goals for student learning.

Keywords: Teacher views of information literacy, Information literacy and active learning, Disciplinary information practices, Information skills, Information literacy and learning.

PROFILE: IMPACT TEACHER

Nancy Pelaez
Associate Professor, Department of Biological Sciences
Purdue University

The introductory biology curriculum is dynamic, and biology faculty members are under constant pressure to innovate in our teaching due to the rapid pace of discovery in the life sciences, to stay abreast of new biological knowledge. However, many students struggle with skills needed for understanding current research, such as defining variables that can be measured, framing questions to investigate observations productively, and processing, visualizing, and interpreting results. Gathering, evaluating, and applying information were foundational practices we expected of students for an authentic educational experience that develops skills required for understanding biological research.

To enhance a lecture course, I collaborated with academic librarians to incorporate peer-led team learning (PLTL) workshops structured to develop biological information literacy as students examined experimental research in an introductory biology course. With PLTL, our students worked together in small groups led by a peer mentor. The students first worked on a weekly problem set individually and then together with a small group in an online meeting room. Each workshop group discussed the problems and prepared to share their findings with the entire class at the next lecture. Because our online peer-lead workshops were recorded, the librarians and I had the chance to observe various factors affecting students and their perceived challenges.

During the first 6 weeks of the semester, students were given practice with information literacy skills as part of the weekly problem set. Each week's information literacy-focused questions were scaffolded, beginning with a skill and building toward having students reflect on and improve their own strategies to inform themselves. In the PLTL environment, students taught one another to be critical and to consider ethical guidelines in using biological information. An example of this arose when a student offered dubious research findings to his group to support a claim. Another student pressed him to learn the source of the research findings, and upon learning that he read it on Wikipedia called on him to trace the research to a primary source.

A review of the small group workshops recorded as online meetings showed that peer leaders made different kinds of interventions, and they sometimes interfered with a group's approach to informing themselves. For example, we observed a peer leader telling students what they were expected to learn, rather than helping students figure things out through discussion and reflection. We also noticed that good prompts from another peer leader helped students make the connection between answering weekly information literacy questions and developing a greater understanding of how biological information has relevance for them personally. Following a review of the small group workshops, we instituted new prompts for peer leaders:

- Did your students explore biological information sources to answer a personal question? If so, give a specific example.
- Did your students use biological information to respond to ideas presented by others or issues of social relevance? If so, how did they inform themselves on the issues?

By observing the workshop recordings, we discovered how to engage students with biological research. We now know what a peer leader should say to prompt a rich discussion. These findings made it possible to reframe the information literacy component to emphasize students' engagement with biological information in personally relevant ways.

6.1 INTRODUCTION

In recent decades, information literacy has grown to become an accepted educational goal for colleges and universities. This growth was largely due to the efforts of the library community (see Behrens, 1994). Addressing its situated and transformative aspects, which place information literacy into a broader context (Lupton & Bruce, 2010), requires integrating information literacy into college or university courses. Academic librarians must form partnerships with teachers, in part, because teachers have the ability to create and make changes to courses. However, an equally important reason to partner with teachers follows from the fact that taking an informed learning approach to information literacy education requires using information to learn course content (Bruce, 2008). Teachers are content experts, yet they may not have experience creating learning activities that involve the intentional use of information. Academic librarians possess considerable knowledge related to how students use information in higher education. While classroom teachers need to take ownership of institutional goals for information literacy, partnering with academic librarians will help them to address effectively those goals in their courses.

As discussed in Chapter 5, partnering to integrate information literacy requires focusing on shared goals (Flierl, Maybee, Riehle, & Johnson, 2016) and speaking a common language (Flierl, 2017). Recognizing that there are different views of information literacy throughout the academy, developing shared goals and approaches also requires academic librarians to be able to determine how potential partners understand information literacy. After providing a brief overview of the research into classroom teachers' views of information literacy, this chapter outlines the findings of a research team at Purdue that investigated how teachers who had completed the Instruction Matters: Purdue Academic Course Transformation (IMPACT) program understood and addressed information literacy in their active learning courses.

6.2 TEACHERS' VIEWS OF INFORMATION LITERACY

Over the last few decades, information literacy has come to be included in the educational accrediting standards of various disciplinary associations in Australia, Canada, the United Kingdom, and the United States (Bradley, 2013). To be compliant, many academic programs or departments have come to be responsible for addressing information literacy. To meet their information literacy-related goals, these programs and departments may welcome partnerships with academic libraries, who are knowledgeable about information literacy and may have experience integrating it into curricula. To partner successfully, classroom faculty and academic librarians must have a shared, or at least similar, understanding of information literacy. The library and information science community have conducted studies to illuminate higher education classroom teachers' perceptions of information literacy.

Some of these studies are less useful than others as they are framed by the ACRL *Information Literacy Competency Standards for Higher Education* (2000). By defining information literacy by the *Standards*, these studies are only able to ascertain how the classroom teachers who are the participants of this research perceive the set of skills outlined in the *Standards* (e.g., Gullikson, 2006; Leckie & Fullerton, 1999; McAdoo, 2008). For example, one such study asked teachers at Canadian universities to rank the importance of 87 information literacy outcomes associated with the five standards (Gullikson, 2006). Within the possibilities presented to them, the participants ranked plagiarism, reading, and restating textual concepts in their own words as the top three information literacy outcomes for higher education students. However, as the study had predetermined the possibilities, the results offer an incomplete picture of how classroom teachers conceptualize information literacy within their teaching contexts or how they expect students to be able to use information.

Another line of research has explored information literacy from the perspective of higher education teachers themselves. To do this, researchers used phenomenography, a research methodology that identifies aspects of people's experiences of phenomena (Marton & Booth, 1997; Marton, Hounsell, & Entwistle, 1997). A growing body of phenomenographic research conducted over the last half century shows that learners studying the same subject may have very different learning experiences depending on a variety of factors, such as what they knew about the subject before the course, how they approach learning, and so forth. Developed in the 1970s, phenomenography was originally used to study students' experiences of learning in educational settings. Eventually, researchers used phenomenography to study teachers' experiences of teaching (e.g., Åkerlind, 2004; Kember, 1997; Prosser & Trigwell, 1999). A subset of this research focused on teachers' experiences of information literacy (Alexandersson & Limberg, 2005; Feind, 2008; Webber & Johnston, 2005; Williams & Wavell, 2007). These studies provide a rich picture of information literacy, showing that it can be understood in various ways even within the same teaching context. This research provides insights that the academic library community can use in promoting and engaging in partnerships with classroom faculty.

The first of these studies was conducted by Christine Bruce (1997), who identified seven different ways that educators in higher education experience information literacy as part of their professional work. The essential elements of the seven experiences are described as interrelated categories:

- Information technology (using information technology for information retrieval and communication);
- Information sources (finding information located in information sources);

- Information process (executing a process);
- Information control (organizing information for future use);
- Knowledge construction (building up a personal knowledge base in a new area of interest);
- Knowledge extension (working with knowledge and personal perspectives adopted in such a way that novel insights are gained); and
- Wisdom (using information wisely for the benefit of others) (Bruce, 1997).

Bruce's (1997) study revealed that while many focus on information skills or processes, higher educators may also perceive information literacy as something more encompassing in which skills or processes are considered just a part of using information to understand and gain insight into a subject, or even to empower change. The findings indicate that the different ways in which information literacy is experienced by higher educators are hierarchically related, meaning that the wisdom category is inclusive of elements of knowledge construction and extension, which are in turn inclusive of elements of the other categories. These research findings challenge conventional skill-focused views of information literacy in higher education. In portraying a richer view of information literacy, the findings from this study call upon educators to consider new approaches to teaching information literacy.

Following Bruce's seminal study, other researchers have investigated teachers' experiences of information literacy and related concepts, such as information seeking or use, in higher education as well as in secondary education (Alexandersson & Limberg, 2005; Feind, 2008; Webber & Johnston, 2005; Williams & Wavell, 2007). In the various contexts in which the studies were conducted, teachers viewed information literacy or information use in a variety of ways. For example, research conducted in the United Kingdom identified differences in higher education English and marketing teachers' experiences of information literacy (Boon et al., 2007; Webber, Boon,& Johnston, 2005). The English academics experienced information literacy in four different ways: (1) accessing and retrieving textual information, (2) using IT to access and retrieve information, (3) possessing basic research skills and knowing how and when to use them, and (4) becoming confident, autonomous learners, and critical thinkers. The marketing academics experienced information literacy in six different ways: (1) accessing information quickly and easily to be aware of what's going on, (2) using IT to work with information, (3) possessing a set of information skills and applying them to the task in hand, (4) using information literacy to solve real-world problems, (5) becoming a critical thinker, and (6) becoming a confident, independent practitioner. Still, there are some generalizable aspects to the findings. As outlined in Table 6.1, there is typically a range in experience, which focuses either on using information generally, or on learning or working in some ways with subject content.

Table 6.1 Foci of educators' experiences of information literacy

Study	Information skills	Subject content
Secondary school	Finding information Comprehend texts Perform information skills	Draw meaning from information Show critical awareness Engage in independent learning
Higher education, general	Information technology Information sources Information process Information control	Knowledge construction Knowledge extension Wisdom
Higher education, English	Accessing and retrieving textual information Using IT to access and retrieve information Possessing basic research skills and knowing how and when to use them	Becoming confident, autonomous learners and critical thinkers
Higher education, marketing	Accessing information quickly and easily to be aware of what's going on Using IT to work with information Possessing a set of information skills and applying them to the task in hand	Becoming a critical thinker Using information literacy to solve real-world problems Becoming a confident, independent practitioner

Data from Bruce, C. S. (1997). *The seven faces of information literacy*. Adelaide: Auslib Press; Webber, S., Boon, S., & Johnston, B. (2005). A comparison of UK academics' conceptions of information literacy in two disciplines: English and marketing. *Library and Information Research*, 29(93), 4–15; Williams, D. A., & Wavell, C. (2007). Secondary school teachers' conceptions of student information literacy. *Journal of Librarianship and Information Science*, 39(4), 199–212.

It is important to note that information skills and practices are perceived as necessary for students to attain. However, there is a dichotomy between teachers who see these skills as an end in themselves versus those who see them as a means to working with and purposefully using content.

Active learning, encouraged in the academy through programs such as IMPACT, may call on students to use information in new ways. In some cases, it may be straightforward to identify how students use information for some types of active learning. For example, problem-based learning may require students to locate and analyze various information sources to inform the ill-defined problem framing their assigned work. However, the ways in which students use information when engaging in other active learning techniques may be less clear. To learn more about how teachers who had gone through the IMPACT program address these concerns in their classrooms, a team of researchers at Purdue studied how teachers view information literacy in relationship to the active learning environments they create in their classrooms (Maybee, Doan, & Flierl, 2016).

6.3 TEACHERS' VIEWS OF INFORMATION LITERACY IN THE ACTIVE LEARNING CLASSROOM

In the study at Purdue, eleven teachers who had all redesigned one of their undergraduate courses through the IMPACT program were interviewed about how they view information literacy (Maybee et al., 2016). The purpose of IMPACT is to make a course more student-centered, which involves having students be more active in the classroom. The researchers were interested in the teachers' perceptions of how students needed to use information to learn through active learning activities. The research question guiding the study was, "How do higher education teachers have their students use information in active learning courses?" The eleven participants, who were from various disciplines, were asked to describe their course redesign and answer three questions related to how they had their students use information:

1. What do you think are the most important things your students need to learn about using information to do well in your IMPACT course?

2. How did you teach the students to use information in the IMPACT course you taught?
3. How has IMPACT changed how you teach your students to use information? (Maybee et al., 2016)

The researchers used thematic analysis procedures adapted from Boyatzis (1998) to analyze the transcribed interviews (Maybee et al., 2016). The three researchers read and coded each of the eleven transcripts. After initial coding, similar codes were clustered into conceptual groupings while continually comparing their thematization to the original transcripts. The analysis was concluded once analytical saturation was achieved, meaning that no new themes emerged from the data. The findings revealed three major themes outlining how participants have their students use information in active learning courses:

- Information Skills You Should Know (students learning information or technology skills)
- Part of the Process of Learning (students engage in information-related activities that lead directly to learning subject content)
- Empowered by Disciplinary Information Practices (students understand and apply disciplinary information practices) (Maybee et al., 2016)

As shown in Table 6.2, five characteristics were identified for each of the three themes, including: (1) how using information is understood, (2) the purpose of learning to use information, (3) the relationship between using information and the subject of the course, (4) what makes learning to use information relevant to students, and (5) what counts as information (Maybee et al., 2016).

Learning activities that align with the theme of Information Skills You Should Know focus on enabling students to learn information or technology skills (Maybee et al., 2016). The learning activities the teachers described using to enable students to learn information skills were not related to learning about the content that was considered the primary focus of the course. For example, the teacher of an introductory evidence-based practice course in nursing had the students complete exercises aimed at learning to search databases and use controlled vocabulary. These teachers' views mirror traditional views of information literacy espoused in higher education that prioritize academic information sources.

Table 6.2 Characteristics of information literacy in active learning environments

Characteristic	Information skills	Process of learning	Disciplinary practices
Using information is…	Skills (information or technology), e.g., learning to use controlled vocabulary	Part of learning strategies	Disciplinary information practices (i.e., using information like a biologist)
Purpose of learning to use information	Use in the course or general academic skill development	Use in the course or beyond	Using information to learn within a disciplinary context
Relationship to the subject of the course	Information skills are taught in separate lessons or assignments, e.g., one shots	Integral (information is used to learn about the subject)	Integral (information is used to learn about the subject)
Relevance to students	Useful skills they will eventually be required to use	Interesting topics (determined by teacher)	Personal interest (determined by teacher or students)
Information is…	Scholarly materials, e.g., peer-reviewed journal articles	Subject to change, dependent on subject-focused learning outcome (e.g., blogs, wikis, standards)	Disciplinary information

Modified from Maybee, C., Doan, T., & Flierl, M. (2016). Information literacy in the active learning classroom. *Journal of Academic Librarianship*, 42(6), 705–711.

In the Part of the Process of Learning theme, using information is considered a part of the active learning activities the teachers used in their courses (Maybee et al., 2016). A variety of active learning activities described by the teachers included using information. Therefore, while students may be learning general information skills, they were learned through activities that were focused on understanding subject content. For example, in a general studies course focused on developing study skills, the teacher had the students share their weekly schedules with a peer group. The students analyzed each other's schedules to determine criteria for the most effective schedule for student academic success. In this situation, the schedules are information sources, and the analysis is a general process that may be transferable to other tasks. However, completing the task leads to subject content-related learning outcomes—in this case, students may grasp the impact of activity choices on academic success.

There is a shift in the Empowered by Disciplinary theme, in which using information is part of better understanding how disciplinary experts, such as biologists, conduct research and report their findings. In this theme, information sources and use are determined by how information is used within the discipline. It should be noted, however, that this does not mean that students are expected to become professionals in the discipline. For example, a teacher of an introductory statistics course wants her students to be able to make use of statistical concepts to evaluate the statistics they encounter in popular media.

6.4 UNDERSTANDING PARTNERS TO BUILD PARTNERSHIPS

This book argues throughout that institutional initiatives in higher education offer opportunities for academic libraries to partner in and contribute to the fulfillment of important learning goals on their campuses. These types of partnerships require that all of those involved see value in what each partner brings to the enterprise. Explaining one's role to partners is easier to do if one can hone their explanation to align with the goals and perspectives of those partners. To advance information literacy, it is important that academic librarians understand how the teachers with whom they are working have their students engage with information. Whether working to help a teacher realize their own instructional vision, or to persuade him or her to take a different pedagogic approach, recognizing a teacher's view of information literacy enables the academic librarian to target his or her efforts.

It is not surprising that there were similarities between the teachers interviewed in the study conducted at Purdue (Maybee et al., 2016), and the prior research into classroom teachers' perceptions of information literacy (Bruce, 1997; Webber & Johnston, 2005; Williams & Wavell, 2007). In all of those studies, the teachers expressed different views of information literacy. Some teachers see information literacy as a set of general skills to be learned independently from other parts of a course's curriculum. Other teachers emphasized an integrated view of information literacy, in which students learn about subject content by using information in some specific way. As discussed in Chapter 2, an integrated approach, because it provides experiences in which information is applied to fulfill a purpose, may be more likely to enable students to use information in other settings (Bruce, 2008).

The Purdue study reveals a more nuanced understanding of how higher education teachers who are taking an integrated approach to information literacy view the role of information in relationship to subject content learning in their courses (Maybee et al., 2016). Teachers whose views align with the Part of the Process of Learning theme have students use information in general ways that lead to learning subject content. Teachers whose views align with the Empowered by Disciplinary Information Practices theme have students learn disciplinary information practices to learn about subject content. The two different approaches might be explained away if the discipline-focused courses were only taken by advanced students. However, all the courses in the study were introductory courses that students typically take during their first or second year of undergraduate studies. Noting that there is a relationship between information literacy and views of learning (Bruce, Edwards, & Lupton, 2006), the Purdue teachers' views of information literacy appear closely related to the way in which they defined the purpose of learning in the course. Teachers whose views align with the Part of the Process of Learning theme were focused on learning within the specific course or to prepare students for future courses. Teachers whose views align with the Empowered by Disciplinary Information Practices theme were focused on students being able to apply what they learned in the courses beyond college.

Using their knowledge of how students use information to learn, academic librarians can coach classroom teachers to consider the benefits of new approaches. For example, academic librarians may work to persuade a teacher who wants to have students learn information skills separately from other course curricula of the benefits to student learning that will result from integrating information literacy into the course holistically. If a classroom teacher intends for students to use information in general ways to learn about subject content, the academic librarian can consider whether it would be advantageous for the students to learn about disciplinary information practices. Armed with the knowledge of how classroom teachers approach having students learn to use information, academic librarians can coach in ways appropriate to the course and institutional context, as well as the classroom teacher's interests and perspective.

6.5 CONCLUSION

The Purdue research project outlined in this chapter describes how classroom teachers view information literacy in the active learning environments they designed through the IMPACT program (Maybee et al., 2016). Additional research into higher education teachers' views of information literacy in various contexts, such as different disciplines or applying specific teaching methods, will inform the academic library community of elements to consider in the development of partnership with classroom teachers. Chapter 7 offers four vignettes that describe collaborations between teachers and librarians involved in the IMPACT program. The chapter concludes by describing a new research project that examined information literacy in courses redesigned through the IMPACT program to student grades, and student perceptions of motivation, the learning environment, and the ability to transfer what they have learned.

REFERENCES

ACRL. (2000). *Information literacy competency standards for higher education.* Chicago, IL: Association of College and Research Libraries.

Åkerlind, G. S. (2004). a new dimension to understanding university teaching. *Teaching in Higher Education, 9*(3), 363–375.

Alexandersson, M., & Limberg, L. (2005). In the shade of the knowledge society and the importance of information literacy. Presented at the 11th Biennial European Association for Research for Learning and Instruction (Earli) Conference, Nicosia, Cyprus. Retrieved from http://InformationR.net/ir/12-1/in_the_shade.html.

Behrens, S. J. (1994). A conceptual analysis and historical overview of information literacy. *College & Research Libraries, 55*(4), 309–322.

Boon, S., Johnston, B., & Webber, S. (2007). A phenomenographic study of English faculty's conceptions of information literacy. *Journal of Documentation, 63*(2), 204–228.

Boyatzis, R. (1998). *Transforming qualitative information: Thematic analysis and code development.* London: Sage.

Bradley, C. (2013). Information literacy in the programmatic university accreditation standards of select professions in Canada, the United States, the United Kingdom, and Australia. *Journal of Information Literacy, 7*(1), 44–68.

Bruce, C. S. (1997). *The seven faces of information literacy.* Adelaide: Auslib Press.

Bruce, C. S. (2008). *Informed learning.* Chicago, IL: American Library Association.

Bruce, C. S., Edwards, S. L., & Lupton, M. (2006). Six frames for information literacy education: A conceptual framework for interpreting the relationships between theory and practice. *ITALICS (Innovations in Teaching and Learning Information and Computer Science), 51*(1), 1–18.

Feind, R. (2008). Results of a phenomenographic investigation of how faculty and staff perceive, engage in, and view information literacy. *The International Journal of Learning, 14*(12), 167–170.

Flierl, M. (2017). Information literacy dialogue as a Wittgensteinian language game: Embedding IL into curricula. In S. Kurbanoğlu, J. Boustany, S. Špiranec, E. Grassian, D. Mizrachi, L. Roy, & T. Çakmak (Eds.), *Information literacy in the inclusive society (communications in computer and information science series): Proceedings of the 4th European information literacy conference* (pp. 687–688). Heidelberg: Springer.

Flierl, M., Maybee, C., Riehle, C. F., & Johnson, N. (2016). IMPACT lessons: Strategically embedding MIL through teacher development in higher education. In D. Oberg & S. Ingvaldsen (Eds.), *Media and information literacy in higher education* (pp. 119–133). Oxford: Chandos.

Gullikson, S. (2006). Faculty perceptions of ACRL's information literacy competency standards for higher education. *Journal of Academic Librarianship, 32*(6), 583–592.

Kember, D. (1997). A reconceptualisation of the research into university academics' conceptions of teaching. *Learning and Instruction, 7*(3), 255–275.

Leckie, G. J., & Fullerton, A. (1999). Information literacy in science and engineering undergraduate education: Faculty attitudes and pedagogical practices. *College and Research Libraries, 60*(1), 9–29.

Lupton, M., & Bruce, C. S. (2010). Windows on information literacy worlds: Generic, situated and transformative perspectives. In A. Lloyd & S. Talja (Eds.), *Practicing information literacy: Bringing theories of learning, practice and information literacy together* (pp. 4–27). Wagga Wagga, N.S.W.: Centre for Information Studies, Charles Sturt University.

Marton, F., & Booth, S. (1997). *Learning and awareness.* Mahwah, NJ: Lawrence Erlbaum.

Marton, F., Hounsell, D., & Entwistle, N. J. (1997). *The experience of learning: Implications for teaching and studying in higher education* (2nd ed.). Edinburgh: Scottish Academic Press.

Maybee, C., Doan, T., & Flierl, M. (2016). Information literacy in the active learning classroom. *Journal of Academic Librarianship, 42*(6), 705–711.

McAdoo, M. L. (2008). *A case study of faculty perceptions of information literacy and its integration into the curriculum* (Ph.D. thesis) Indiana University of Pennsylvania, Indiana, PA.

Prosser, M., & Trigwell, K. (1999). *Understanding learning and teaching: The experience in higher education.* Philadelphia, PA: Society for Research into Higher Education and Open University Press.

Webber, S., Boon, S., & Johnston, B. (2005). A comparison of UK academics' conceptions of information literacy in two disciplines: English and marketing. *Library and Information Research, 29*(93), 4–15.

Webber, S., & Johnston, B. (2005). Information literacy in the curriculum: Selected findings from a phenomenographic study of UK conceptions of, and pedagogy for, information literacy. In C. Rust (Ed.), *Improving student learning: Diversity and inclusivity. Proceedings of the 11th ISL symposium* (pp. 212–224). Birmingham: Oxford Brookes Univ.

Williams, D. A., & Wavell, C. (2007). Secondary school teachers' conceptions of student information literacy. *Journal of Librarianship and Information Science, 39*(4), 199–212.

CHAPTER 7

Information Literacy in IMPACT Courses

Contents

Abstract

This chapter provides four vignettes outlining collaborations between the teachers and librarians involved in the IMPACT program to integrate information literacy into courses at Purdue. The projects described are from foundational courses in statistics, technology, science communication, and biology. Although the educational offerings described in the vignettes differ widely, each has some of the characteristics of informed learning. Following the vignettes, a new research project is introduced that examines data from 102 course sections redesigned through the IMPACT program revealing the relationship of aspects of information literacy to student grades, as well as student perceptions of motivation, the learning environment, and their ability to transfer what they have learned.

Keywords: Librarian and teacher collaboration, Information literacy activities, Informed learning activities, Information literacy in disciplinary courses, Information literacy research

PROFILE: IMPACT TEAM MEMBER

Nastasha Johnson
Physical and Mathematical Sciences Information Specialist
Purdue University Libraries

IMPACT Learning
https://doi.org/10.1016/B978-0-08-102077-7.00007-0

In 2014, I received a grant from Assessment in Action (AiA), an Institute of Museum and Library Services (IMLS) funded national assessment program offered by the Association of Institutional Research, Association of Public Land Grant Universities, and the Council of Independent Colleges. The overarching purpose of AiA was to assist libraries in articulating their value within the entire University community. Many of the colleges and universities that participated in the 3-year program investigated specific classes or services, which they thought would be good examples of how the library impacts the success of students. At Purdue University, we selected a course in the Purdue Polytechnic Institute that offered an introduction to the engineering design process. The course also met the University's core curriculum information literacy outcome.

For the AiA project, three information literacy-related assignments were evaluated. For the first and second assignments, students are asked to identify and define a design problem in a campus cafeteria. An important part of the design process is to define the problem and find out what issues exist from a design perspective. These issues can be human, product, or service related. Additionally, students in the course mimic what design engineers do by determining what solutions already exist before designing a new solution. Solutions can exist within academic settings, or outside of academia. Students need to explore various kinds of information, such as academic journals, technical reports, government documents and reports, or proprietary or company sources, to find solutions to their problem. For the third assignment, students report their design process and research findings for a problem and solution of their choice in a presentation and report. For the AiA project, we evaluated the quality of the sources in each of the three assignments.

As part of the first assignment, students are asked to watch a video about navigating the library website, searching two databases, and selecting keywords. In the video they are also taught how to evaluate sources for quality using the CRAP test. After watching the video, they had to create an annotated bibliography with citations and source evaluation. After completing the first assignment, a librarian comes in and reviews some of the same material that was demonstrated on the video and answers any questions pertaining to their first assignment. After the visit, students are asked to complete a similar second assignment, once any concerns or questions they had about the first assignment have been addressed. About seven weeks later the students are asked to write and present a paper about a problem and solution of their own design, which is the third assignment. My team was able to determine that there was growth in source quality from the video to after the librarian visit. We also determined that students were able to sustain the growth several weeks later until their final project and paper.

From the AiA work, we have been able to articulate the value of scaffolded information literacy instruction, and a variety of delivery methods, as well as librarian involvement in course design. Additionally, from the work we were able to understand the quantifiable library impact, and not just qualitative. There's a lot more work to be done, but this work has been a great foundation for more assessment work to come. It was also impactful to work directly with the departments served, and institutional research colleagues in developing the project design.

7.1 INTRODUCTION

This chapter begins with four vignettes that provide a glimpse into the collaborations between teachers and librarians involved in the IMPACT program. The stories of these partnerships all involve integrating information literacy into courses. To varying degrees, each project, be it the redesign of a course, or creating or changing an assignment, can be identified with some of the characteristics of informed learning (Bruce & Hughes, 2010). One of the things that is notable when reading the vignettes is the differences between each of the collaborative efforts. The first vignette presents the story of a librarian working with a statistics teacher and an instructional technologist to create a social media assignment. The second describes a technology course in which students use information to inform a design process. The third vignette illustrates how a communication course benefited when a librarian used the *Framework for Information Literacy for Higher Education* (ACRL, 2015) to prompt discussions with the teacher about the nature of information literacy. The fourth vignette describes how two librarians and a biologist used an information literacy framework to make students see the relevance of information literacy exercises.

Following the qualitatively rich stories of collaborations between librarians and teachers described in the vignettes, a new research project is introduced that investigates information literacy in a significant number of courses redesigned through the IMPACT program. Using data from surveys with students and teachers, the study relates information literacy to student grades as well as student perceptions of motivation, the learning environment, and the ability to transfer what they have learned.

7.2 IMPACT VIGNETTES

7.2.1 Applying Statistical Literacy in Facebook Conversations

Ellen Gundlach, a statistics teacher at Purdue who participated in the IMPACT program in 2012, redesigned a 400-student, introductory-level statistical literacy course primarily taken by liberal arts majors. This course is part of the university core curriculum, meeting both the information literacy and the science, technology, and society foundational core outcomes. To address students' varying learning needs, Gundlach created new online and hybrid sections of the course, while adding active learning activities to the traditional lecture section (Gundlach, Richards, Nelson, & Levesque-Bristol, 2015). The goal of this class is not for students to learn statistical calculations, but rather to enable them to become informed consumers of the statistics they encounter in their daily lives.

After completing the IMPACT program and implementing the redesigned version of the course, Gundlach continued to meet regularly with the members of her IMPACT team, who included Kevin O'Shea, a staff person from Purdue's ITaP unit, and Clarence Maybee, a Libraries faculty member. Together, this group developed an assignment intended to teach students to evaluate statistical information to learn about a topic of interest to them (Gundlach, Maybee, & O'Shea, 2015). The assignment allowed students to practice using concepts learned earlier in the course to evaluate statistical information found in popular media, such as statistics from research studies reported in a news article, video, or podcast. The assignment provided students an experience of a learning environment similar to real-life to discuss their conclusions; the students were required to share the news item they selected, and their analysis of the statistics described in it, in posts on Mixable, a social media platform developed at Purdue. A closed system in which only the Purdue community can participate, Mixable is similar to Facebook, with which the group anticipated students would be familiar.

After posting a link to the news item in Mixable, each student had to create a post discussing various aspects of the statistics described in the article, video, or podcast (Gundlach, Maybee, et al., 2015). They also had to advance the discussion by making four "statistically intelligent" comments on some of their peers' posts. The students were provided with examples of acceptable and unacceptable comments, and encouraged to make comments grounded in the concepts they learned about in the course, such as how the data was collected, possible lurking variables, and whether there were potential ethical or bias issues.

The assignment is an example of integrating information literacy into disciplinary coursework. As outlined in Table 7.1, the assignment has several of the characteristics associated with informed learning (Bruce, 2008). Informed learning suggests that information is anything that is informing, which within the context of this assignment are the statistics reported in research findings. Incorporating the dual focus that is an essential characteristic of informed learning, the assignment encouraged the students to deepen their awareness of statistical concepts (course content) by applying those concepts in the

Table 7.1 Informed learning aspects of the statistics assignment

Characteristics	Description
Engaging with information	Evaluating statistics
Course content	Statistical concepts
Information	Statistics from research studies reported on in the popular press
Pedagogy	Social media peer-discussion
	Learners apply statistical concepts learned previously
	Codeveloped by a statistics teacher, an information technologist, and a librarian
Transformative change	Learners adopt a more critical stance when encountering statistical information in their daily lives

evaluation of statistical data (information literacy) in a social media environment similar to ones they may use in their personal lives.

In 2013, students were given a survey asking them about their experience of the social media assignment (Gundlach, Maybee et al., 2015). The results of the survey (response rate of 96.2%, $n = 405$) suggest that the assignment provided a positive experience for the students. However, the results of the survey also showed a difference in the ways students approached the assignment. While some searched for topics of interest, such as chocolate or weight loss, over 50% of the students searched for specific statistical terms such as, "research studies" or "experiment," (53.2%). To encourage student engagement in the assignment, Gundlach decided in future iterations of the assignment to place more emphasis on students being able to find a topic of interest.

7.2.2 Informed Design in a Technology Course

A group of four teachers participating in the IMPACT program during the summer of 2012 redesigned an introductory technology course. This course is a requirement for most of the students in the Purdue Polytechnic Institute. The course is also part of the university core curriculum, meeting both the information literacy and the science, technology, and society foundational core outcomes. Before the teachers' participation in IMPACT, the course was taught through lecture, with over 600 students congregating in a lecture hall in the fall semester and over 300 in the spring semester. After IMPACT, the course changed to a model in which it was separated into smaller sections with 40 students in each. The redesigned version of the course employs active learning techniques, with students participating in groups to investigate problems and to design potential solutions.

After redesigning the course in IMPACT, one of the teachers on the team, Nathan Mentzer, assumed the role of coordinator of the course. In this role, he set the curriculum and oversaw the teachers of the various sections. The librarian who had been part of the IMPACT team for this course had left the university, and another Purdue librarian, Nastasha Johnson, began working with the course. Johnson received an Assessment in Action (AiA) grant from ACRL to assess information literacy in the course (see Profile). In 2014, she began teaching a section of the course. Johnson became an integral part of the course team. Johnson worked closely with Mentzer and the other teachers to enhance learning within the course, including leading efforts to develop the information literacy assignments.

In this introductory technology course, students learned five steps of a design thinking process for solving problems in technology and engineering: (1) definition, (2) articulation, (3) ideation, (4) evaluation, and (5) communication; using information is a part of each step (Flierl, Maybee, Riehle, & Johnson, 2016). Students in the course are introduced to the design process by observing a campus location and identifying issues and potential technological solutions. For example, one semester students were sent to watch automobile and pedestrian traffic flow at a busy intersection on Purdue's campus. The students had to identify issues, such as pedestrians crossing against the traffic lights, or cars going faster than permitted, and brainstorm solutions. After observing the site, students explored the scholarly literature for similar issues and to determine existing solutions.

Learning about the design process, including gathering and analyzing information to inform the process, was reinforced in a larger design project (Flierl et al., 2016). Teams of students identified a topic and began their investigation of it. They collected data to define a problem through observations or interviews. For example, students investigating issues related to food service for students on campus might observe students and staff in one of the dining halls. Students also explored the scholarly literature to examine the research related to their topic, as well as investigating literature outlining possible solutions. The student teams presented their designs and design process to the class at the end of the semester.

The coursework in this introductory technology course is an example of informed learning (Flierl et al., 2016). Outlined in Table 7.2, the students learned to find and use scholarly sources and collect and analyze original data (information literacy) to inform a design process (course content). Aligned with the informed learning idea that information consists of whatever is informing (Bruce, 2008), information in the learning context of the course included both scholarly articles and analyzed data collected through first-hand observations or interviews. In contrast to the statistics course, which had students apply disciplinary tools to enrich personal communication, the technology course asked students to engage in information practices they will use as technology professionals.

Table 7.2 Informed learning aspects of the technology course

Characteristics	Description
Engaging with information	Analyzing original data and scholarly information to inform design
Subject content	Design process
Information	Scholarly articles, technical reports
Pedagogy	Learners using information to inform design is scaffolded across the course
	Codeveloped by a team that was led by technology teacher, and included a librarian
Transformative change	Learners adopt a professional perspective

7.2.3 Communicating Scientific Information

A communication teacher, Melanie Morgan, participated in the IMPACT program in 2013. She redesigned a course that focused specifically on scientific communication. The course is required for students in Purdue's College of Science. This course is also part of the university core curriculum, meeting the oral communication foundational core outcome. The course aims to enable students to communicate scientific and technical information to various audiences effectively. For many of the students, the communication practices they learn in the course support them in their future academic or professional lives as scientists (Flierl et al., 2016). The science communication course was different than the courses described in the other vignettes in that a focus on information literacy was an integral part of the course before Morgan became a participant in the IMPACT program.

Catherine Fraser Riehle, at that time the Libraries' liaison to Purdue's School of Communication, along with other members of the IMPACT team, worked with Morgan to redesign the course. Course assignments typically required students to gather and evaluate information to integrate into presentations (Flierl et al., 2016). The assignments were scaffolded so that the students engaged with information more complexly across the semester. Early assignments had students engage with information resources with which they would likely be familiar, such as Google, Wikipedia, science news, and blogs. Building on what students learned earlier in the course, later assignments focus on students gathering and evaluating information from specialized resources, such as Google Scholar, and disciplinary research databases to inform their presentations. While students prepared for presentations they also explored concepts, such as authority and scholarly community, related to communicating as a scholar.

Riehle realized that as Morgan thought through redesigning the course, many of her interests were things that were being discussed in the academic library community (Flierl et al., 2016). At this time, the committee that was preparing the *Framework for Information Literacy for Higher Education* (ACRL, 2015) was sharing drafts for academic librarians to provide feedback. Riehle began sharing the drafts with Morgan, which led to rich conversations about information literacy, and what aspects of it should be focused on in the course (Flierl et al., 2016). As their conversations evolved, Morgan began to consider how the teachers facilitating the different sections of the course may be addressing information literacy differently, and how she could assess the impact on student learning that might result from these variations.

Outlined in Table 7.3, the assignments in the communication course may be associated with some characteristics of informed learning (Bruce, 2008). In this course, students learn communication practices (course content) to communicate scientific information to different audiences, which involves gathering, evaluating, and analyzing scholarly articles, technical reports, news and other popular sources (information literacy; Flierl et al., 2016). Appropriate for this context, the information students engage with includes scholarly materials and other items typically used by scientists presenting at academic conferences or other venues. While the course is not intended

Table 7.3 Informed learning aspects of the science communication course

Characteristics	Description
Engaging with information	Evaluating and communicating scientific information
Course content	Communication practices
Information	Scholarly articles, technical information
Pedagogy	Scaffolded presentations
	Draws from students' prior experiences using information
	Librarian and teachers explore information literacy model

to transform students' views of themselves, the students are learning communication practices associated with a being a scientist, which may prompt them to consider their role as future scientists.

7.2.4 Making Biological Information Literacy Relevant

Another example of integrating information literacy into a course that was redesigned through IMPACT comes from an introductory biology course. The teacher, Nancy Pelaez, had participated in the IMPACT program in 2011. The course, comprised of about 50 students, was using a peer-led team learning approach in which students completed homework tasks individually and then discussed problematic aspects of the homework in small groups of four students, led by a team mentor. The student group then shared their consensus answers during class, getting feedback from the teacher and other students.

In 2012, Pelaez began working with two IMPACT librarians, Maribeth Slebodnik and Clarence Maybee. Slebodnik was the liaison to biology, and Maybee was an information literacy specialist. Before working together, Pelaez had added information literacy activities to the course in the form of homework assignments that students would complete. Students were required to find biological information and analyze research articles. The students applied what they learned when preparing and presenting an end-of-semester academic poster. The goal was for students to become aware of how biologists answer questions relevant to the field, and begin to adopt the perspective of a biologist. However, Pelaez felt that the students were not grasping the relevance of the information literacy exercises. When Pelaez and the two librarians first convened, it was to develop the homework exercises further. However, all three members of the group had attended a workshop facilitated by the Australian information literacy researcher, Christine Bruce, held at Purdue in August of 2012, which led their work in a new direction.

Bruce's workshop discussed applying the Six Frames of Information Literacy model to teaching and learning in higher education. The model, described in a scholarly article (Bruce, Edwards, & Lupton, 2006), outlines how views of teaching and learning frame ideas related to information literacy. The model proposed that information literacy can be viewed in six different ways:

1. Content frame—learning information concepts and skills
2. Competency frame—developing a set of information competencies

3. Learning to Learn frame—using information like a professional
4. Personal Relevance frame—related to personal goals
5. Social Impact frame—supportive of societal good
6. Relational frame—a complex of varying ways of interacting with information

Reflecting on Bruce's workshop, Pelaez realized that her students in the introductory biology course were likely viewing the information literacy exercises in the course as intended to help them gain necessary competencies rather than to use information more like a biologist. The students did not perceive the exercises as helping them to meet personal goals or address societal needs. Pelaez and the librarians brainstormed about how the coursework could be changed to enable the students to relate the information literacy aspects of the course to their interests or desires to improve society.

The homework exercises remained very similar because of departmental needs to not make the redesigned section of the course too different from the traditional sections also offered. However, at the beginning of the semester, the students in the redesigned version of the course were required to identify something personal to them that could be informed by engaging with biological information. The topics students chose were wide ranging, with one student investigating alcoholism in the hopes of understanding a relative with that disease, and another exploring herbal medicine, saying that he had always wanted to learn more about it. After making the modifications, the teacher was satisfied that the students understood the relevance of completing the information literacy-focused homework assignments.

In contrast to coursework designed with other teachers who had participated in IMPACT, Pelaez was knowledgeable of the Six Frames of Information Literacy model (Bruce et al., 2006), which is one of the frameworks that underpin informed learning (Bruce, 2008). With the goal of exposing students to ways in which biologists use information to reach conclusions, the information that was appropriate for the students to use in this context was scholarly journal articles. Outlined in Table 7.4, the students were learning how to find and evaluate biological information (information literacy) to learn biological concepts (course content) applicable to their interests.

Table 7.4 Informed learning aspects of the biology assignment

Characteristics	Description
Engaging with information	Using information like a biologist
Course content	Biological facts, concepts, and theories
Information	Scholarly articles
Pedagogy	Peer-led team discussions
	Learners selection of a topic based on personal experiences
	Codeveloped by a biology teacher, and two librarians
Transformative change	Learners adopt a disciplinary perspective

7.3 NEW PROJECT: INFORMATION LITERACY, MOTIVATION, AND LEARNING GAINS

While the vignettes provide detailed descriptions of information literacy collaborations resulting from Purdue Libraries' involvement in IMPACT, this section outlines a project to examine information literacy across the courses redesigned through the IMPACT program. Three librarians involved with IMPACT—Mike Flierl, Clarence Maybee, and Rachel Fundator—are partnering with Emily Bonem, an instructional developer working with CIE, to study how information literacy in these courses relates to students' grades, and student perceptions of motivation, the learning environment, and their ability to transfer what they have learned.

The idea of this project began in 2015 when Purdue Libraries were able to add information literacy-focused questions to a survey that teachers who had participated in the IMPACT program receive, asking them to report on different aspects of their redesigned courses. The questions on the survey focus on a variety of course elements, such as time spent lecturing versus facilitating active learning, the application of pedagogic strategies (e.g., problem-based or case-based learning), and the use of educational technologies. Using a 5-point Likert scale ranging from "never or rarely" (0–5 times a semester) to "often" (more than 16 times a semester), the information literacy questions on the survey ask the teachers how often they have students in their redesigned course:

- Pose questions or problems that require further investigation
- Access information outside of assigned readings and tasks
- Evaluate information sources
- Synthesize information and communicate the results through a deliverable (e.g., project, paper, homework, etc.)
- Apply conventions of attribution (e.g., cite, reference, paraphrase, quote, etc.)

The information literacy questions added to the survey were adopted from a list of fundamental skills comprising the criteria for courses meeting Purdue's core curriculum foundational information literacy outcome. Drawing from the Association of American Colleges and Universities' (AACU, 2009) *Information Literacy Value Rubric*, the list of skills defines foundation-level information literacy at Purdue. With the core curriculum approved by the University Senate in 2012, the list of skills provides a shared definition of information literacy agreed upon by Purdue faculty.

The research team recognized that we could relate the data collected from the survey of teachers who participated in IMPACT program to data collected from university records and perception surveys of the students enrolled in those courses. To date, there have not been large-scale investigations examining the impact of information literacy on learning gains at the course level. Past studies examining the relationship between information literacy and learning gains or other educational concepts, such as student motivation, have usually examined student performance at the assignment level. Studies have also explored the impact on student success metrics, such as GPA, and general use of information, such as the use of library resources or services (e.g., Soria, Fransen, & Nackerud, 2014).

Data were collected across the 2015–16 academic year. The sample included 102 course sections in which at least 15 students and at least 25% of the students enrolled in the course had responded. 3152 students (46%) completed the student perceptions survey. The survey included measures of learning climate, basic psychological needs, self-determined motivation and perceived knowledge transfer scales. The initial analysis suggests that how students engage with information, and the frequency with which they do so, can positively or negatively correlate with both student learning and motivation. In particular, synthesizing and communicating information correlated with greater learning and motivation than other activities, such as accessing information or applying conventions of attribution. The research team plans to publish the full results of this study in the coming year.

7.4 CONCLUSION

The current chapter provides examples of information literacy collaborations that have resulted from participation in the IMPACT program. While the individual projects were very different from each other—some focusing on the redesign of an entire course, and others on developing a particular assignment—they all shared some of the characteristics of informed learning (Bruce & Hughes, 2010). A new research project is also described in this chapter that examines information literacy in a significant number of courses that were redesigned through the IMPACT program and relates that to student grades and student perceptions of motivation, the learning environment, and their ability to transfer what they have learned. Chapter 8 will outline two endeavors in which a theory and model used in the IMPACT program were drawn together with ideas from informed learning to create new information literacy tools.

REFERENCES

AACU. (2009). Information literacy value rubric. Association of American Colleges and Universities. Retrieved from http://www.aacu.org/value/rubrics/information-literacy.

ACRL. (2015). Framework for information literacy for higher education. Association of College and Research Libraries. Retrieved from http://www.ala.org/acrl/standards/ilframework.

Bruce, C. S. (2008). *Informed Learning*. Chicago, IL: American Library Association.

Bruce, C. S., Edwards, S. L., & Lupton, M. (2006). Six frames for information literacy education: A conceptual framework for interpreting the relationships between theory and practice. *ITALICS (Innovations in Teaching and Learning Information and Computer Science)*, *51*(1), 1–18.

Bruce, C. S., & Hughes, H. (2010). Informed learning: A pedagogical construct for information literacy. *Library and Information Science Research*, *32*(4), A2–A8.

Flierl, M., Maybee, C., Riehle, C. F., & Johnson, N. (2016). IMPACT lessons: Strategically embedding MIL through teacher development in higher education. In D. Oberg & S. Ingvaldsen (Eds.), *Media and information literacy in higher education* (pp. 119–133). Oxford: Chandos.

Gundlach, E., Maybee, C., & O'Shea, K. (2015). Statistical literacy social media project for the masses. *The Journal of Faculty Development*, *29*(2), 71–80.

Gundlach, E., Richards, K. A. R., Nelson, D., & Levesque-Bristol, C. (2015). A comparison of student attitudes, statistical reasoning, performance, and perceptions for web-augmented traditional, fully online, and flipped sections of a statistical literacy class. *Journal of Statistics Education*, *23*(1).

Soria, K. M., Fransen, J., & Nackerud, S. (2014). Stacks, serials, search engines, and students' success: First-year undergraduate students' library use, academic achievement, and retention. *The Journal of Academic Librarianship*, *40*(1), 84–91. https://doi.org/10.1016/j.acalib.2013.12.002.

CHAPTER 8

Using Theories From IMPACT to Create Informed Learning Tools

Contents

Abstract

This chapter describes how librarians involved in the IMPACT program have been able to draw from the theories and models they were introduced to in the program to develop information literacy scholarship. Two examples of these endeavors are presented in the chapter. In the first example, self-determination theory is drawn together with informed learning to create a model for developing motivating learning activities that enable learning course content through engagement with information. The second example draws informed learning together with concepts borrowed from backward design to create a new instructional design model called informed learning design. Informed learning design provides a process for determining the key elements such as learning outcomes, assessment, and learning activities, of a course developed using an informed learning approach to information literacy.

Keywords: Self-determination theory, Backward design, Informed learning design, Instructional design, Motivation and information literacy

PROFILE: IMPACT TEAM MEMBER

Michael Flierl
Learning Design Specialist
Purdue University Libraries

IMPACT Learning
https://doi.org/10.1016/B978-0-08-102077-7.00008-2

Starting in 2014, I had the good fortune to work in Instruction Matters: Purdue Academic Course Transformation (IMPACT) as an information literacy instructional designer. At first, I attempted to learn as much as possible about self-determination theory, backward design, informed learning, and other theories related to teaching and learning. I had three semesters of experience teaching introductory philosophy classes during and after my first master's degree, but my theoretical understanding of teaching and learning was lacking.

I hope that one could understand my original inclination to view information literacy theory as distinct from other theories, including self-determination theory. It was unintuitive to me at a theoretical level to connect a theory concerning student perceptions of psychological needs with an information literacy theory focused on learning subject content. Pragmatically, I was also concerned that a teacher participating in IMPACT could get confused if we discussed multiple theories at once, or in relation to one another. Redesigning a class is difficult enough without having to learn about theory from multiple fields. While I did not view the various theories discussed in IMPACT as competing with informed learning per se, I did not view them as complimentary either.

After becoming more knowledgeable and experienced in self-determination theory and informed learning, I found myself seeing stronger and stronger relationships between self-determination theory and informed learning. In IMPACT, we try to shift the teacher's perspective towards a more student-centered one, where they are more concerned with *what students are learning* rather than *what they are teaching*. It is a subtle but important shift. An activity or assessment that was once thought to be essential can suddenly be tossed aside. A similar shift occurred in my own thinking. I needed to be more IMPACT teacher-centric. How could I help a teacher think about the ways students engage with information in the context of their class? In hindsight, this is painfully evident. If information use is as ubiquitous as information literacy theory states, then why not discuss information through a lens that resonates with a teacher? Put another way, many teachers are concerned with motivating students to learn. Why not leverage this opportunity to discuss information literacy? Informed learning could go beyond even being complimentary to other theories; it could be synergistic.

Pragmatically, this allowed me to work more effectively with teachers participating in IMPACT. I could now more adroitly find a common ground on which to have meaningful conversations about student motivation and information use. Self-determination theory could be abstract and theoretical. How students use information in the class is concrete. I found it useful to discuss how, through more intentional engagements with information, students could feel more autonomous (in choosing the information they use), competent (in using information like an expert in the field), and related to the course content (by choosing how to interact with information). Self-determination theory refined my own understanding of informed learning and instructional design. Informed learning not only works well with other theories, it thrives in doing so.

8.1 INTRODUCTION

Teaching and learning initiatives are typically guided by ideas about how to enhance student learning in higher education. Sometimes such initiatives are grounded in one or more specific learning theories or models, such as experiential learning, competency-based learning, or authentic learning. Even if an initiative is not formally associated with a specific theory of teaching and learning, such ideas are implicitly understood by those involved. If they want to be involved, academic librarians must become conversant in the theories and models underpinning a teaching and learning initiative.

In a major initiative such as the IMPACT program at Purdue, there may be several educational theories and models that come together to guide the program' goals and implementation. The key idea that underpins the IMPACT program is "student-centered learning," which aims to reorient teaching decisions to focus purposefully on what enables students to learn (Barr & Tagg, 1995). The instructional design model, backward design, provides a process that focuses attention on important aspects of a course, that is, learning outcomes, assessment, and learning activities (Wiggins & McTighe, 2005). Drawing from the work of the National Center for Academic Transformation (NCAT) (Twigg, 2003), the IMPACT program originally focused on choosing a course model, such as hybrid, fully online, or flipped. Since 2013, the program has drawn from self-determination theory (Ryan & Deci, 2000) to highlight the importance of student motivation in fostering student success.

The librarians participating on teams have to become familiar enough with each of the educational theories and models that guide the IMPACT program to apply them in their work with the teachers as they redesign courses. The librarians have reported that they often use the ideas they learned about through participating in the program in their other teaching and learning efforts on campus. For example, after being introduced to team-based learning by a scholar the IMPACT program brought to campus, one librarian involved in the program described applying elements of a team-based learning model to an undergraduate course she co-taught on exploring great issues in science.

The librarians have also been able to draw from theories and models they were introduced to in the IMPACT program to inform their information literacy scholarship. Two examples of these endeavors are presented in this chapter. In the first, self-determination theory (Ryan & Deci, 2000) is drawn together with informed learning (Bruce, 2008) to create a model for developing motivating learning activities that enable learning course content through engagement with information. The second example draws informed learning together with concepts borrowed from backward design (Wiggins & McTighe, 2005) to create an informed learning design model.

8.2 SELF-DETERMINATION THEORY AND IMPACT

In 2013, Purdue hired Chantal Levesque Bristol to be the new director of the institution's Center for Instructional Excellence. Bristol began working closely with the IMPACT program. Drawing from her background in psychology, she recommended to the IMPACT management team that they consider "motivation" as the key actor in enabling student learning. Specifically, she recommended "self-determination theory," which suggests that there is a relationship between self-determination and different forms of motivation (Ryan & Deci, 2000, 2017). Ideally, higher education students would be intrinsically motivated to learn for their own personal satisfaction and achievement. However, most educators would agree that the majority of college and university students are not, at least not in every course, intrinsically motivated. Some forms of extrinsic motivation can enable students to become self-determined learners. In their efforts to support student learning and overall success, higher education teachers can create learning environments that encourage these forms of extrinsic motivation.

There are four kinds of extrinsic motivation: external regulation, introjection, identification, and integrated regulation (Ryan & Deci, 2000). External regulation and introjection are not associated with self-determined behaviors. Students that are motivated by external regulation feel that their actions are overly controlled, while students motivated by introjection only engage in actions to avoid feeling guilty or anxious. Identification and integrated regulation are associated with self-determination. Students that are motivated by identification see an action as personally significant, while students motivated by integrated regulation have internalized the need for that action. Students who are able to internalize extrinsic goals for learning move closer to being intrinsically motivated. Self-determination theory suggests that to be motivating, learning activities need to satisfy three interrelated psychological needs:

- autonomy (volition over what they do)
- relatedness (connected to others)
- competence (able to succeed) (Ryan & Deci, 2000)

To meet these three psychological needs, students need to perceive that they are able to make appropriate choices regarding what they learn and how they approach their learning (Ryan & Deci, 2000). Students also need to feel connected to the teacher and other students. This does not mean that teachers need to be overly friendly with their students, but that students perceive the teacher genuinely cares that they are able to learn. The students also must perceive that they can successfully accomplish the learning tasks. Learning environments which support these psychological needs are associated with student dedication and engagement (Vansteenkiste, Simons, Lens, Sheldon, & Deci, 2004), as well as academic achievement (Guay, Ratelle, & Chanal, 2008).

The librarians, instructional developers, and technologists work with teachers in the IMPACT program to create learning environments that enable students to feel they have choices, are connected, and confident in their ability to succeed in the course. When self-determination theory was first introduced, the librarians working with the program had to develop ways to communicate its usefulness to the teachers participating in the IMPACT program. In the beginning, the librarians were essentially learning about self-determination theory along with the teachers and developers participating in the IMPACT program. Overtime, the librarians gained a deeper understanding of self-determination theory, and how to use it in partnering with teachers to create motivating learning environments for students.

8.3 MOTIVATING INFORMED LEARNERS

After self-determination theory was introduced into the IMPACT FLC meetings in 2013, it became a major foundation of the program. While the weekly meeting topics remained the same, the facilitators would frequently draw the three psychological needs of autonomy, relatedness, and competency that are a part of self-determination theory (Ryan & Deci, 2000) into the weekly discussions. For example, on the week in which the meetings focused on assessment practices, the facilitator would ask the participants how they thought students would perceive different kinds of assessment, such as repeatable quizzes, peer grading, and so forth, in regards to autonomy, relatedness, and competency. Maybee and Flierl, two librarians who work closely with the IMPACT program, became interested in the relationship between informed learning and self-determination theory. Specifically, the two librarians were interested in how informed learning activities, which emphasize the role of information in the learning process (Bruce, 2008), could be made more motivating by considering the three psychological needs of autonomy, relatedness, and competency.

Maybee and Flierl's efforts were originally directed toward drawing connections between information literacy and student motivation for the teachers participating in the IMPACT program. In exploring self-determination theory for their work in the IMPACT program, the two librarians noticed similarities with informed learning. For example, both informed learning and self-determination theory emphasize the agency of the students, rather than of the teachers, as key for enabling learning (Maybee & Flierl, 2017). The two librarians came to recognize that self-determination theory, and more specifically the three psychological needs of autonomy, relatedness, and competency, could support the development of motivating informed learning activities. Drawing from informed learning and self-determination theory, Maybee and Flierl (2017) produced a model for creating such activities. They presented their paper outlining the model at the European Information Literacy Conference (ECIL) in Prague in 2016.

Informed learning activities should reflect the principles that guide the informed learning pedagogy (Bruce & Hughes, 2010). Therefore, the activities would need to: (1) build on students' prior experiences, (2) focus simultaneously on learning to use information and on course content, and (3) enable students to experience using information and subject content in new ways. Grounded in the characteristics of the approach, informed learning activities would likely have students actively engaging with information. The information the students use to learn could be anything, so long as it is informing. This may include using disciplinary information and learning about disciplinary information practices. For example, a political science course may have students engage with census and polling data, while a landscape design course might expose students to topographical maps and weather data. Ensuring that an informed learning activity is motivating, it must address the three basic psychological needs of autonomy, relatedness, and competency described previously (Ryan & Deci, 2000).

Academic librarians and teachers can use the framework outlined in Table 8.1 to develop motivating learning activities, in which information is used to foster the learning of course content. Designing informed learning activities that are motivating first involves determining how course content is to be learned through engagement with information. Then, these two elements are examined through the lens of the three basic psychological needs of autonomy, relatedness, and competency. The specific information sources and the ways information may be used to learn about the topic will vary within a given learning situation.

A hypothetical example of the redesign of an undergraduate historical research methods course for second-year undergraduates will help show how the three psychological needs relate to using information, and the influence this may have on learning course content. Before the course was redesigned, the students in this course were

Table 8.1 Relating self-determination theory to informed learning

Informed learning	Self-determination theory		
	Autonomy	Relatedness	Competency
Course content learning	Student perceives choices in what they learn	Student feels connected to the subject content and/ or peers/ teacher	Student feels capable of learning subject content
Engagement with information, e.g., academic, disciplinary, or professional information practices	Student perceives options in how they use information to learn	Student feels connected to students, teacher, and/ or subject material through intentional engagement with information	Student feels capable of using information in the way needed to learn

From Maybee, C., & Flierl, M. (2017). Motivating learners through information literacy. In S. Kurbanoğlu, J. Boustany, S. Špiranec, E. Grassian, D. Mizrachi, L. Roy, & T. Çakmak (Eds.), *Information Literacy in the Inclusive Society (Communications in Computer and Information Science Series): Proceedings of the 4th European Information Literacy Conference* (pp. 698–707). Heidelberg: Springer.

required to write a paper using methods learned in class on any topic they chose. However, the students often had difficulty selecting an appropriate topic. In this case, the students may have had too much autonomy, which as pointed out by Maybee and Flierl (2017), can influence how they were able to engage with the information they needed to learn. The class toured the university archive, but using archival materials in their final paper was optional. This could impede students' ability to feel connected to the information and information practices with which they were engaging. Like many undergraduates (Head & Eisenberg, 2010), the students in the history course were able to find information on their topic, but had difficulty determining which articles to use and how to synthesize them in the paper.

To motivate the students, the teachers of the historical research methods course designed a new final project. They had students make short videos about an historical event at the university. This limited the choice of topics to events with which the students likely had some familiarity. Students' interest in the history of the institution they were attending made them feel more connected to what they were researching for their documentary. The students now saw the relevance of the class visit to the archives, which grew into a workshop to prepare them to use archival documents and images. The archivist made herself available to consult with the students about finding archival materials for their projects. The teachers arranged to have two workshops with staff from the educational technologies unit to teach students the technical aspects of producing the videos. The class watched documentary films together, and discussed the different approaches taken to historical documentation. To help students feel competent in using and synthesizing sources to communicate effectively in their videos, the teachers held workshops. In the workshops, the teachers advised students on techniques used for historical documentary, and the librarians helped the students in their use of sources. Through this project, the students were motivated to learn about historical research methods while also engaging with and learning to use archival materials.

8.4 BACKWARD DESIGN AND IMPACT

The IMPACT program is guided by a backward design instructional design model developed by Wiggins and McTighe (2005). The model was used by the working group at Purdue in the development of the 13-week IMPACT curriculum in 2012. By drawing attention to important aspects of a course, the design model provides a focused process for redesigning courses. The IMPACT meetings that occur across the 13 weeks are structured to focus first on developing or revising course learning outcomes, which drive the creation of an assessment plan and determining learning activities. Discussed in Chapter 5, backward design supports the work of the librarians and faculty and staff from CIE and ITaP in their work to redesign courses with the teachers participating in the IMPACT program.

Many instructional design models, sometimes called curriculum design models, were developed to make occupational training programs more effective and efficient. For example, the ADDIE model was designed by Florida State University for use in training programs by the United States Army (Branson et al., 1975). ADDIE stands for "Analysis, Design, Development, Implementation, and Evaluation", which are the steps of the design process. The ADDIE design process begins by considering aspects of the learning environment, such as identifying learner characteristics, delivery options, and constraints imposed by the environment on the intended learning. ADDIE has been adapted specifically for use by librarians, resulting in the "Blended Librarians Adapted ADDIE Model," or BLAAM (Bell & Shank, 2007). Offering a similar list of steps to ADDIE, the Dick and Carey model emphasizes a systems view, suggesting that the various elements, such as the teacher, learners, materials, instructional activities, delivery system, and assessment components, must be understood holistically (Dick, Carey, & Carey, 2009).

In contrast to other instructional design models, backward design was specially created for use in higher education (Wiggins & McTighe, 2005). Backward design inverts the stages that are usually part of other instructional design models. In the three stages of the design process, teachers develop:

(1) learning outcomes,

(2) assessment, and

(3) learning activities (Wiggins & McTighe, 2005).

The backward design process begins with determining what students are intended to know or do after the completion of the instructional unit (Wiggins & McTighe, 2005). While it is acknowledged that the process may not always be linear, meaning teachers may revisit the different stages as they work to design a course, it is important that the goals for learning are defined before determining assessment and learning activities. The learning outcomes, which identify what students are intended to know or be able to do as a result of instruction, drive the development of assessment and learning activities.

Backward design is different than other instructional design models in additional ways as well. Less concerned with issues of efficacy and cost-effectiveness, the main objective of the backward design process is fostering student learning (Wiggins & McTighe, 2005). Rather than placing an emphasis on what is to be taught, backward design focuses on what is to be learned. Wiggins and McTighe suggest that teaching activities should enable what they term *enduring understanding*. They suggest that this type of learning may result in *transferability*, allowing learners to apply their newly gained understanding to their work in other contexts.

8.5 INFORMED LEARNING DESIGN

Exposure to the backward design model (Wiggins & McTighe, 2005) and the benefits of using it with teachers to redesign courses through the IMPACT program led Maybee to recognize how it could be applied to support the practical application of an informed learning approach to information literacy in the higher education classroom. As a result, he and some of his colleagues are using aspects of backward design and other educational theories to develop a new instructional design model for informed learning. The new model, called "informed learning design," provides a process for determining the key elements of courses and coursework grounded in an informed learning approach to information literacy (Bruce et al., 2017).

As with the motivated informed learning activities model described above, informed learning design is grounded in the three principles that guide informed learning: (1) build on students prior experiences, (2) focus simultaneously on learning to use information and course content, and (3) enable students to experience using information and subject content in new ways (Bruce & Hughes, 2010). The design model also draws from the variation theory of learning, which suggests that there are selected aspects of what a teacher wants the class to learn about that students must become aware of in order for their learning to align with the teacher's intentions (Marton, 2014; Marton & Tsui, 2004). In an informed learning environment, learning would involve becoming aware of aspects that relate to both information literacy and course content (Maybee, Bruce, Lupton, & Rebmann, 2017).

Drawing from the backward design idea that goals for learning must be identified before developing other aspects of a course (Wiggins & McTighe, 2005), informed learning design follows a series of stages similar to those used in the backward design process. That is, goals for learning are identified first, and are used to determine assessment and learning activities. The three stages of informed learning design are:
- Identifying critical aspects of intended learning, which include both using information and course content.

- Defining assessment methods for gauging students' increased awareness of critical aspects associated with using information and course content.
- Determining activities that enable students to learn about critical aspects associated with course content by intentionally using information (Bruce et al., 2017).

During Stage 1, a teacher using the informed learning design model to design a course would examine past teaching experiences or conduct an initial evaluation to identify students' current experiences. The teacher uses that information to determine goals for learning that reflect changes in students' awareness of using information and course content. In Stage 2, the teacher develops a plan for assessing the changes in students' awareness at the end of the course, but also at key points throughout. In Stage 3, the learning activities are selected. The learning activities must enable students' awareness and abilities to use information to learn in the ways defined by the goals for learning identified in Stage 1. Once the class begins, the teacher can use the results of the periodic assessment to make adjustments to the learning activities, to ensure students are able to learn as intended.

A brief overview of the informed learning design model has been shared in a paper describing new scholarly directions related to informed learning that was included in the 10-year anniversary edition of the *Journal of Information Literacy* (Bruce et al., 2017). Maybee and Flierl also conducted a workshop for instructional developers that focused on using the design model to develop informed learning activities at the 2016 Professional and Organizational Development (POD) Conference held in Louisville, Kentucky. The research team, comprised of Maybee, Christine Bruce, and Mandy Lupton from Queensland University of Technology, and Ming Fai Pang from The University of Hong Kong, anticipate that a paper describing informed learning design in fuller detail will be published in late 2017.

8.6 CONCLUSION

This chapter highlights some of the benefits of librarians participating in campus initiatives in which they are introduced to educational theories and models. Beyond being able to apply them in other teaching and learning situations, such theories and models can be drawn upon to develop new information literacy educational tools. Shared through scholarship, these new tools may impact the information literacy educational practices at other institutions. Concluding Part 2 of this book, Chapter 9 shifts away from describing aspects of librarians' participation in the IMPACT program, to reflect instead on the lessons learned from involvement in the program.

REFERENCES

Barr, R. B., & Tagg, J. (1995). From teaching to learning: A new paradigm for undergraduate education. *Change, 27*(6), 12–25.

Bell, S. J., & Shank, J. D. (2007). *Academic librarianship by design: A blended librarian's guide to the tools and techniques.* Chicago: American Library Association.

Branson, R. K., Rayner, G. T., Cox, J. L., Furman, J. P., King, F. J., & Hannum, W. H. (1975). Interservice procedures for instructional systems development (5 vols.). (No. TRADOC Pam 350-30 NAVEDTRA 106A; NTIS No. ADA 019 486 through ADA 019 490). Ft Monroe, VT: Army Training and Doctrine Command.

Bruce, C. S. (2008). *Informed learning.* Chicago, IL: American Library Association.

Bruce, C. S., Demasson, A., Hughes, H., Lupton, M., Sayyad Abdi, E., Maybee, C., et al. (2017). Information literacy and informed learning: Conceptual innovations for IL research and practice futures. *Journal of Information Literacy, 11*(1), 4–22. https://doi.org/10.11645/11.1.2184.

Bruce, C. S., & Hughes, H. (2010). Informed learning: A pedagogical construct for information literacy. *Library and Information Science Research, 32*(4), A2–A8.

Dick, W., Carey, L., & Carey, J. O. (2009). *The systematic design of instruction* (7th ed.). Upper Saddle River, NJ: Merrill/Pearson.

Guay, F., Ratelle, C. F., & Chanal, J. (2008). Optimal learning in optimal contexts: The role of self-determination in education. *Canadian Psychology, 49*(3), 233–240. https://doi.org/10.1037/a0012758.

Head, A. J., & Eisenberg, M. (2010). Truth be told: How college students evaluate and use information in the digital age (project information literacy research report). University of Washington's Information School. Retrieved from http://projectinfolit.org/publications/.

Marton, F. (2014). *Necessary conditions for learning.* New York: Routledge.

Marton, F., & Tsui, A. (2004). *Classroom discourse and the space of learning.* Mahwah, NJ: L. Erlbaum Associates.

Maybee, C., Bruce, C. S., Lupton, M., & Rebmann, K. (2017). Designing rich information experiences to shape learning outcomes. *Studies in Higher Education, 42*(12), 2373–2388.

Maybee, C., & Flierl, M. (2017). Motivating learners through information literacy. In S. Kurbanoğlu, J. Boustany, S. Špiranec, E. Grassian, D. Mizrachi, L. Roy, & T. Çakmak (Eds.), *Information literacy in the inclusive society (communications in computer and information science series). Proceedings of the 4th European Information Literacy Conference.* (pp. 698–707). Heidelberg: Springer.

Ryan, R. M., & Deci, E. L. (2000). Intrinsic and Extrinsic Motivations: Classic Definitions and New Directions. *Contemporary Educational Psychology, 25*(1), 54–67. https://doi.org/10.1006/ceps.1999.1020.

Ryan, R. M., & Deci, E. L. (2017). Self-determination theory: An introduction and overview. In *Self-determination theory: Basic psychological needs in motivation, development, and wellness.* New York: Guilford Press. (pp. 3–25).

Twigg, C. (2003). Improving learning and reducing costs: New models for online learning. *EDUCAUSE Review, 38*(5), 28–38.

Vansteenkiste, M., Simons, J., Lens, W., Sheldon, K. M., & Deci, E. L. (2004). Motivating learning, performance, and persistence: The synergistic effects of intrinsic goal contents and autonomy-supportive contexts. *Journal of Personality and Social Psychology, 87*(2), 246–260. https://doi.org/10.1037/0022-3514.87.2.246.

Wiggins, G. P., & McTighe, J. (2005). *Understanding by design* (2nd ed.). Alexandria, VA: Association for Supervision and Curriculum Development.

CHAPTER 9

Lessons Learned in IMPACT

Contents

Abstract

This chapter outlines three lessons learned by the librarians involved in the IMPACT program working with teachers to integrate information literacy into coursework using an informed learning approach. One of the lessons learned was that the librarians concentrating their efforts on advocating for information literacy was unproductive. The second lesson learned was that focusing on the challenges teachers face often leads to discussions of how information literacy might enhance student learning. The third lesson learned was that navigating discussions about information literacy with teachers required the librarians to recognize the teachers' views of information literacy. The lessons learned by Purdue librarians involved in the IMPACT program may provide insights to librarians working with teachers on other campuses to integrate information literacy into courses.

Keywords: Information literacy advocacy, Information literacy collaboration, Librarian and teacher collaboration, Teacher views of information literacy, Information literacy integration

PROFILE: IMPACT TEAM MEMBER

Rachel Fundator
Information Literacy Instructional Designer
Purdue University Libraries

I believe that information literacy plays an important role in advancing disciplinary learning. However, I learned from the insights of veteran librarians, and personal experience, not to be overzealous when proposing information literacy activities to the teachers involved in the Instruction Matters: Purdue Academic Course Transformation (IMPACT) program. Teachers may not see the connection between learning and information literacy and may feel off-put by my suggestions. I find that meaningful discussions about information literacy do occur when they are relevant to a teacher's situation.

I learned the effectiveness of this approach with my first IMPACT team, which was comprised of a group of assistant professors from engineering. During a meeting about the challenges their students have completing assignments, the conversation shifted to the varied ways the students use statistics and algorithms to solve engineering problems. It was a successful moment to introduce spontaneously information literacy, as the teachers initiated and collectively analyzed how engineering students need to use information. Subtle questions from the support team members helped the teachers consider their individual expectations of how engineering students should engage with information and how those expectations align with the students' use of information in class.

I rarely use the term "information literacy" in the conversations we have about using information in IMPACT. I was initially concerned that the absence of the words "information literacy" meant that I was not sufficiently demonstrating the important role information plays in the learning process. I now find implicit discussions about using information to be substantive and valuable when I see that they help teachers reflect upon and reconsider how they approach teaching.

My interactions with the teacher of a residential design course exemplifies this lesson. One of our conversations gradually shifted to a thought-provoking discussion about how the various information resources and practices students engaged with throughout the course helped them accomplish different tasks. While most assignments introduced students to residential design by having them interpret inclusive design documentation and design, critique, and present floor plans, the final project gave them authentic practice as residential designers, as they interviewed clients and responded to their design needs. We never used the term "information literacy," but this was a valuable interaction, as the teacher recognized that the various information practices and resources he incorporated into his course could help students learn the different aspects of being a residential designer.

My involvement in IMPACT has taught me that I do not need to have an explicit discussion about "information literacy" to advocate for teaching students to use information purposefully in ways supportive of learning outcomes. In fact, approaching information literacy with subtlety and focusing on the value of how students use information as part of learning are two lessons that I have transferred to my interactions with disciplinary teachers outside of IMPACT. These lessons allow me to have realistic expectations about my discussions of information literacy in which I aim to help teachers take ownership of the information practices that students engage with in their courses.

9.1 INTRODUCTION

Purdue Libraries has been able to contribute strongly to Purdue's goals for teaching and learning through the creation and continued participation in the IMPACT program. While the gains for the Libraries and the institution have been significant, there have been occasional challenges to work through. Such challenges can often be learning experiences. Detailed below, the librarians working with the IMPACT program increasingly found that advocating information literacy to teachers before there is a need for it can be unproductive. Instead, they realized that focusing on the challenges teachers face often opens the door to discussions of how information literacy might enhance student learning. However, they also found that, although sometimes implicit, in order to navigate discussions with teachers the librarians needed to recognize their teachers' views of information literacy. Learning about the challenges they faced, and how the librarians involved in the IMPACT program overcame them, can provide insights to librarians working with teachers on their campuses to enhance learning and to integrate information literacy into courses.

9.2 DON'T ENGAGE IN UNPRODUCTIVE ADVOCACY

The librarians have found that espousing the benefits of information literacy to the teachers participating in the IMPACT program does not usually work well. Instead, they have learned to wait until a need emerges that information literacy may help address. The eight Purdue librarians preparing to participate in the IMPACT program in 2012 were aware that they should not initially be too assertive about their ideas for information literacy when working with the teachers. The group met several times to discuss what they hoped to accomplish through their involvement in the IMPACT program. They also strategized about how to best approach their work on IMPACT teams. Aligned with the strategy suggested by Iannuzzi (1998), the librarians turned to the IMPACT program's mission statement to inform their approach:

> Redesign foundational courses by using research findings to create student-centered teaching and learning environments.

In support of the mission of IMPACT, the group of librarians concluded that they should focus their efforts on creating student-centered learning. As it was not directly part of the mission, the librarians would not advocate for information literacy to be part of courses. However, if the need for information literacy activities in a course being redesigned through the program arose as part of team discussions, the librarian on the team would make suggestions. While the primary role of the librarians on the team (as well as the instructional developers and technologists) was to work with the teacher participating in IMPACT to enhance pedagogy, librarians looked for opportunities for integrating information literacy.

Although the academic librarians working on IMPACT teams were not explicitly advocating for information literacy, in 2012 and 2013 a librarian did present a session about the importance of information literacy at one of the weekly meetings. Before attending the session, IMPACT teachers read the "Six frames for information literacy education: A conceptual framework for interpreting the relationships between theory and practice" (Bruce, Edwards, & Lupton, 2006). This article describes how views of information literacy are associated with views of teaching and learning.

In one session, one of the teachers participating in IMPACT told the facilitator that the "Six Frames" (Bruce et al., 2006) article was not relevant to his work in IMPACT. He continued to say that the article outlined things that he believed the librarians wanted him to do with his class, but did not align with what he perceived to be necessary changes in his course. Of course, this exchange only represented the views of one participant. However, it did align with other feedback received at this time suggesting that the program needed to focus less on design and learning theories generally, and instead introduce teachers participating in IMPACT to specific ideas aimed at helping them address specific course issues.

Information literacy continues to be discussed at one of the IMPACT meetings. However, rather than presenting a general over-view, teachers participating in the program are asked to consider how their students need to use information to complete their course-work, and if the students are capable of using information in this way at the beginning of the course. If they believe that the students are not capable, the teachers are asked to determine what learning activities need to be added to the course so that students can learn to use information in the ways necessary to prepare them for their coursework.

9.3 FOCUS ON THE CHALLENGES FACED BY TEACHERS

In the early days of the IMPACT program, the FLC meetings of-ten focused on learning about educational theories and models that might inform a teacher's work in the classroom. The faculty and staff working with and developing the program recognized that the teach-ers involved were not greatly interested in learning design and learn-ing theories, but rather wanted to solve issues and enhance learning in their classrooms. In response to this perceived need, the IMPACT management group focused the work of the faculty learning commu-nity to center on identifying and resolving classroom concerns. The IMPACT curriculum shifted to become more problem focused.

Early on in the program, the teachers are asked to identify their goals for their participation in IMPACT. The goals they identify be-come the subject of discussions and activities that are part of the weekly meetings. The shift to focus on teaching and learning chal-lenges faced by the teacher drives the work of IMPACT teams. The change to more of the redesign work happening within IMPACT teams resulted in the librarians adopting the coaching approach to working with teachers participating in IMPACT, as described by Flierl and his colleagues (2016). The approach emerged naturally amongst the academic librarians working with the program and was later compared to existing models (Frank, Raschke, Wood, & Yang, 2001; Vickers, 1992), identifying some overarching strategies. Being at the table when teachers are considering making major changes to a course has often led to information literacy being integrated into the course, and in some cases becoming a major focus of the course.

One disadvantage of the team approach is that librarians may work with a course in which there is little or no opportunity to integrate information literacy. In the early years of the program, teams were comprised of a librarian, an instructional developer, an instructional technologist, and one teacher. A team of four redesigning a single Purdue course limited the opportunities for information literacy. It should be noted, of course, that making the course more student-centered is achieving an important institutional goal. In 2013, the IMPACT team model was changed to have three teachers and a librarian, an instructional developer, and an instructional technologist on each team. Information literacy was a component of the redesign for at least one of the three courses, which afforded more opportunities for the librarians participating in IMPACT.

In discussing challenges faced by teachers, librarians may be able to suggest solutions that involve integrating information literacy into a course. The vignettes in Chapter 8 describe some of the outcomes of such discussions. An example is the biologist who wanted her students to see the relevance of using information in a biology context. Once the librarians understood the teacher's concern, they worked with the biologist to brainstorm solutions. The solution they settled on was having the students identify something personal to them that could be informed by engaging with biological information. The students used that topic as they worked through homework assignments that taught them to use biological information.

9.4 NEGOTIATE VIEWS OF INFORMATION LITERACY

When teachers are interested in information literacy, academic librarians must be attentive to the teachers' views of information literacy and learning. The teachers, faculty, and staff from CIE and ITaP working with the IMPACT program acknowledge that the librarians are information literacy experts. Nevertheless, the teachers and others on the team do have a way that they conceptualize information literacy, even if they are not explicitly aware of it. For this reason, if a librarian puts forth their perspective on information literacy and how it will enhance student learning, it may be rejected. Therefore, the librarians do not assert their views of information literacy, but instead, work through a process in which the teacher and other members of the team come to a shared understanding of the role information literacy plays in the redesigned course.

The teachers participating in IMPACT understood information literacy in various ways that align with the functional, situated, and to a lesser degree, the critical descriptions of information literacy described in the "GeST Windows" article authored by Lupton and Bruce (2010). Some teachers participating in IMPACT expressed views of information literacy in which it was framed as a set of information skills. As was found in research into university educators' experiences of information literacy (Webber, Boon, & Johnston, 2005), it is possible that some teachers participating in IMPACT felt that information literacy was not their responsibility. However, some teachers viewed information literacy as a set of information skills and address it as such in their courses (Maybee, Doan, & Flierl, 2016).

Rather than being truly integrated, teachers with an information skills understanding of information literacy would offer information literacy activities that were separate from the primary content of their course (Flierl et al., 2016). That is, these teachers may provide online tutorials to cover specific information skills or invite librarians to conduct a lesson on using Purdue Libraries' information resources. In an effort to foster informed learning in such a course, an academic librarian working with one of these teachers would spend time encouraging the teacher to see the connection between information literacy and content-focused learning goals.

In contrast, other teachers conceptualize information literacy as closely linked to their learning goals for the course they were redesigning. For example, some of the teachers interviewed about the role of information literacy in their redesigned course talked about students learning to use information to compete and learn from classroom exercises or out-of-class assignments (Maybee et al., 2016). Academic librarians working with these teachers would focus on improving how students engage with information to enhance content-focused learning through these exercises (Flierl et al., 2016). Other teachers interviewed in the study wanted their students to learn disciplinary information practices to either engage with discipline knowledge or apply disciplinary tools to learn outside of the discipline. The courses redesigned by these teachers had information literacy-focused learning outcomes. The efforts of Purdue librarians working with such courses focus on developing learning activities and an assessment strategy to enable students to achieve the learning outcomes.

The approach the librarians took in working with teachers who viewed information literacy as situated within disciplinary practices took many forms. Exemplified in the vignettes discussed in Chapter 8, in some cases librarians worked with teachers to identify disciplinary information practices they wanted students to learn and then develop assignments and lessons to enable students to learn those practices. For example, the librarians working with the introductory technology course worked with the course coordinator and other teachers to determine what kinds of information students needed to aid them in identifying technological problems and compare existing solutions (Flierl et al., 2016). The librarian led the group in the development of assignments for the students to learn to find and analyze this information.

In other cases, librarians were able to draw from theoretical models put forth by the library and information science community (Flierl et al., 2016). For example, the librarian working with the science communication course shared the *Framework for Information Literacy for Higher Education* with a teacher participating in IMPACT to foster discussions of how information literacy relates to and could support students learning the disciplinary practices associated with communicating scientific information. The librarians working with the biologist used the "Six frames" article (Bruce et al., 2006) to inform the design of instruction aimed at enabling students to make personal connections through using information. Beyond having the students make a personal connection, one of the librarians used the "Six Frames" to suggest that the students consider the social benefits of using biological information to investigate a topic through the lens of biology.

9.5 REFLECTIONS ON LESSONS LEARNED

Working with teachers to integrate information literacy into a course using an informed learning approach requires a great deal of flexibility.

Adopting this approach necessitates understanding many things about the course, the teacher, and the students before being able to suggest changes that would be impactful. Librarians working in this way have a lot to juggle. There is no way to know at the start of working with a teacher if this effort will lead to information literacy being introduced into the course. As the example of the teacher who did not find the "Six Frames" (Bruce et al., 2006) article relevant to his work outlines, explaining the benefits of information literacy may not lead to a collaboration.

Yet, there is the other story in which, after listening to the biologist's concerns about how to make information literacy relevant to her students, the librarians introduced the "Six Frames" to inform a solution. This case drives home the point that focusing on classroom problems can provide a way into collaborations about information literacy and its impact on learning. The vignettes in Chapter 8 provide examples of what such collaborations can achieve for student learning. Sometimes the librarians involved in the IMPACT program lament the amount of time that needs to be set aside for IMPACT meetings. Yet, they also recognize that the conversations taking place at these meetings can result in otherwise unobtainable collaborations with the teacher that will help student learning through meaningful engagement with information.

9.6 CONCLUSION

This chapter highlights three lessons learned by librarians participating in the IMPACT program. An important takeaway from these lessons is that building relationships resulting in collaboration requires librarians to listen to teachers' concerns about issues they may be having in their classrooms. Understanding these issues allows librarians to show how information literacy may help address those needs.

Chapter 10 is the first chapter in Part 3 of this book. Part 3 discusses how the ideas presented in Parts 1 and 2 may inform efforts to integrate information literacy on other higher education campuses using an informed learning approach. Building on the lessons learned outlined in this chapter, Chapter 10 suggests three essential elements of information literacy efforts necessary for advancing informed learning (Bruce, 2008).

REFERENCES

Bruce, C. S. (2008). *Informed learning*. Chicago, IL: American Library Association.

Bruce, C. S., Edwards, S. L., & Lupton, M. (2006). Six frames for information literacy education: A conceptual framework for interpreting the relationships between theory and practice. *ITALICS (Innovations in Teaching and Learning Information and Computer Science), 51*(1), 1–18.

Flierl, M., Maybee, C., Riehle, C. F., & Johnson, N. (2016). IMPACT lessons: Strategically embedding MIL through teacher development in higher education. In D. Oberg & S. Ingvaldsen (Eds.), *Media and information literacy in higher education* (pp. 119–133). Oxford: Chandos.

Frank, D., Raschke, G., Wood, J., & Yang, J. (2001). Information consulting: The key to success in academic libraries. *Journal of Academic Librarianship, 27*(1), 90–96.

Iannuzzi, P. (1998). Faculty development and information literacy: establishing campus partnerships. *Reference Services Review, 26*(3/4), 97–102.

Lupton, M., & Bruce, C. S. (2010). Windows on information literacy worlds: Generic, situated and transformative perspectives. In A. Lloyd & S. Talja (Eds.), *Practicing information literacy: Bringing theories of learning, practice and information literacy together* (pp. 4–27). Wagga Wagga, N.S.W.: Centre for Information Studies, Charles Sturt University.

Maybee, C., Doan, T., & Flierl, M. (2016). Information literacy in the active learning classroom. *Journal of Academic Librarianship, 42*(6), 705–711.

Vickers, P. (1992). Information consultancy in the UK. *Journal of Information Science, 18*, 259–267.

Webber, S., Boon, S., & Johnston, B. (2005). A comparison of UK academics' conceptions of information literacy in two disciplines: English and marketing. *Library and Information Research, 29*(93), 4–15.

Reenvisioning Information Literacy Education

PART 3

Reenvisioning
Information Literacy
Education

CHAPTER 10

Three Essentials for Integrating Information Literacy

Contents

Abstract

This chapter describes three key elements necessary for advancing an informed learning approach. First, information literacy needs to be viewed as part of learning. When information literacy is understood to be part of learning, it follows that it needs to be integrated into courses in a way that allows students to use information to learn course content. To integrate information literacy into curricula, academic librarians must partner with teachers, who are able to make changes to courses. To locate teachers receptive to such changes, the second element necessary for advancing an informed learning approach is that academic librarians must identify where conversations about improving teaching and learning are taking place on their campuses. The third key element necessary for advancing an informed learning approach in higher education is developing collaborations with teachers.

Keywords: Information literacy integration, Information literacy and learning, Teaching and learning innovation, Teaching and learning initiatives, Librarian and teacher collaboration.

10.1 INTRODUCTION

The Instruction Matters: Purdue Academic Course Transformation (IMPACT) program provides an example of how academic librarians have integrated information literacy into courses when working with teachers to create learning environments that are more student-centered. Drawn from both the scholarly literature outlined in Part 1, and Purdue Libraries' experiences working with the IMPACT program described in Part 2, this chapter outlines recommendations for academic libraries undertaking an informed learning approach to advancing information literacy at their colleges and universities.

There are three key elements necessary for advancing an informed learning approach (see Fig. 10.1). First, information literacy needs to be viewed as integral to the learning process. When using information is understood as a part of learning (Bruce, 2008), it becomes clear that information literacy needs to be integrated into courses in a way that allows students to use information to learn course content. The ways students use information is closely related to what they can learn about the content (Limberg, 1999; Maybee, Bruce, Lupton, & Rebmann, 2017). For some teachers, this will seem obvious, while others may need to be convinced. The best time to discuss how information literacy can improve content-focused learning outcomes is when teachers are considering making changes to a course. Therefore, the second key element involves academic librarians identifying where conversations about improving teaching and learning are taking place on their campuses.

The third key element necessary for advancing an informed learning approach is developing collaborations with teachers. As discussed in Chapter 9, one lesson learned by the librarians participating in the IMPACT program is that espousing the benefits of informed learning may not be the best approach to convincing teachers to integrate information literacy into coursework. Many teachers may be resistant to ideas that do not align with their views of information literacy, and more importantly, their views of what might improve learning in their course. In developing collaborations, academic librarians need to

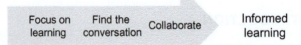

Fig. 10.1 Necessary elements for advancing informed learning on college and university campuses.

approach such discussions carefully, first listening to teachers' concerns, and when appropriate, suggesting how learning outcomes could be enhanced through engagement with information.

10.2 FOCUS ON STUDENT LEARNING

Information literacy is closely related to learning. Even the ACRL (2000) *Standards* alluded to this idea, defining an information-literate individual as someone who can, among other things, incorporate selected information into their knowledge base. The information literacy efforts that most closely align with the *Standards* typically involve academic librarians teaching students information skills that include such things as defining problems, finding and evaluating information, and so forth. While these are not unimportant things to learn, when taught in this way, information skills are separated from the context in which they would normally be applied. This was exemplified by the teacher in a nursing program who redesigned a course through the IMPACT program that had students attend a lesson on searching for materials, although that activity was not directly related to any of their other coursework (Maybee, Doan, & Flierl, 2016). The programmatic efforts in higher education designed to teach information skills make information literacy the thing to be learned. From this perspective, information literacy becomes a content of its own, rather than an integral part of learning about something else (Lupton, 2008).

The approaches discussed at the beginning of the book show that information literacy may be viewed as situated within the practices of a community (Lloyd, 2010), or as part of a critical lens through which one can reveal social and political aspects of the world (Tewell, 2015). The fire fighters in one of Lloyd's (2007) studies provide an extreme example of situated information literacy. When working to put out a fire, the fire fighters gauge their safety by analyzing the information their bodies provide about the heat coming through their suits. A tamer example from higher education can be drawn from one the vignettes in Chapter 8 in which students in a technology course redesigned through the IMPACT program learn a design process that involves using information to identify design problems and solutions (Flierl, Maybee, Riehle, & Johnson, 2016). Students exploring a topic from a critical perspective would be asked to identify the people who benefit from the production of information found on the subject, and the people who are not represented (Simmons, 2005). In contrast to learning activities such as these, many of the current efforts in higher education do not place information literacy into contexts that allow students to learn to use information in ways that are meaningful to them.

The academic library community is poised to change their approach to information literacy in higher education. It is likely that the information skills approach to information literacy that dominated higher education for over half a century may come to be considered the first phase. In this period, academic libraries were able to develop the necessary groundwork to bring information literacy to its current level of acceptance in higher education. ACRL's (2015) *Framework for Information Literacy for Higher Education,* with its broader conceptualization of information literacy, provides a framework that academic librarians could use for their efforts in the second stage. Comprised of the six frames: (1) Scholarship is a Conversation, (2) Research as Inquiry, (3) Format as Process, (4) Authority is Constructed and Contextual, (5) Searching as Exploration, and (6) Information has Value, the *Framework* certainly provides a larger view of information literacy that aligns with many of the efforts undertaken in academia. However, if information can be anything that is informing (Bruce, 2008), then the *Framework's* construction of information literacy could still be limiting when one considers all of the ways that teachers and students may use information in the context of learning.

Addressing criticisms of the information skills approach (Kapitzke, 2003; Pawley, 2003; Whitworth, 2014), information literacy efforts must focus on teaching students to use information in context. In higher education, the context for using information would likely be a learning context. Using information can be considered a part of learning, but even more than that, the two can be seen as interacting with one another (Kari & Savolainen, 2010). This interaction was present in Limberg's (1999) study of high school students whose understanding of the topics they researched about the creation of the European Union were closely related to their awareness of different aspects of seeking information. That is to say, students who experienced a greater complexity in how they found information understood their topics with more sophistication as well. The study of an upper-level writing course in which the students were asked to trace the development of a language and gender issue across time revealed that the specific way the teacher had the students engage with information influenced what they were able to learn about their topics (Maybee, Bruce, et al., 2017).

It is this interaction between learning and information literacy that demands the adoption of a new approach to information literacy in higher education. Although further investigation of the relationship between information literacy and learning is required, the evidence suggests that the ways in which students use information influences how they learn (Limberg, 1999; Maybee, Bruce, et al., 2017). Educators may improve learning outcomes by attending more carefully to how students interact with information as they learn in a course. Through both research and teaching experiences, academic librarians continue to explore how students use information as part of the learning process. Informed learning offers an approach to information literacy in higher education that focuses on using information to learn about course content (Bruce, 2008). Drawing from the knowledge of how students engage with information, academic librarians are uniquely positioned to work with teaching colleagues to develop coursework that improves learning through the intentional use of information.

10.3 FIND THE CONVERSATION

Academic librarians and teachers need to work together to teach students ways of using information that support the various goals that are part of a higher education curriculum. Librarians' knowledge of how students use information as part of the learning process can inform the development of assignments and lessons designed to allow students to learn to use information as they engage with course content (Bruce, 2008). Purdue librarians' experiences in the IMPACT program suggest that teachers who are considering pedagogic changes are more likely to be open to discussions of how their students need to be able to use information. Academic librarians should seek out venues on their campuses in which teachers and staff are exploring educational innovations. In such venues, teachers are focused on improving or enhancing student learning.

Some academic librarians already work in close collaboration with teachers. For them, the shift to an informed learning approach to integrating information literacy may involve new conversations with existing partners focused on how learning gains can improve by changing how students use information in a course. However, many academic librarians have less contact with teachers. For these librarians, integrating informed learning into courses using an informed learning approach begins with finding ways to have conversations with teachers. Of course, there may also be teachers on college and university campuses that are specifically interested in information literacy.

An example of a teacher interested in information literacy is provided in the vignette in Chapter 7 that describes a biologist who worked with Purdue librarians to make information literacy homework exercises more relevant to students. That teacher wanted to partner with librarians because she believed that their collaboration would enable significant learning for the students in her course. Sometimes academic librarians can work with such teachers individually to integrate information literacy into their coursework. If there is enough interest, academic libraries may consider creating an initiative that specifically aims to support teachers to integrate information literacy into their courses. An example is the initiative to integrate information literacy into courses at all levels of the undergraduate curriculum at Trinity University, which had institutional support from the highest levels of the university (Millet, Donald, & Wilson, 2009).

However, many higher education teachers are not interested in integrating information literacy into their courses. These teachers may express a variety of reasons why information literacy should not be included in their course. They may believe there is no room in the course to cover such material, or that students should learn to use information somewhere else (Webber, Boon, & Johnston, 2005), such as basic composition or introductory communication. While some teachers will never come to see its importance, others may embrace integrating information literacy into a course if they can be made to see how it supports learning in their courses. There are teachers who participated in the IMPACT program who came to understand the value of information literacy through discussions that took place over the 13 weeks of their involvement.

Purdue Libraries' 6-year involvement with the IMPACT program demonstrates that partnering with teachers in a faculty development program that is not specifically about information literacy can still provide opportunities for integrating it into university courses. A teaching and learning initiative that specifically focuses on information literacy, such as the one at Trinity University (Millet et al., 2009), would have been attended by teachers interested in integrating information literacy into their courses. It would not have been likely to attract teachers who had never thought about what their students might gain from learning how to use information in their course. Teachers in the IMPACT program focus on making their courses more student-centered. The academic librarians working with the teachers via IMPACT teams brought up the topic of teaching students how to use information when it was a means to accomplishing course goals for learning. The librarians working with IMPACT were able to convince teachers to be more intentional in how their students use information.

Possible venues for academic libraries to consider when determining where the "conversation" about teaching and learning may be taking place on their campuses include the teaching and learning initiatives outlined in Chapter 3. The initiatives discussed in that chapter include first-year seminars and experiences, residential learning communities, writing across the curriculum, service learning opportunities, online learning, undergraduate research, capstone experiences, and faculty development programs. However, the proper venue could also be created by a smaller, less formal effort. For example, Dan Guberman, an instructional developer for Purdue's Center for Instructional Excellence, has arranged informal groups to read and discuss recent books that outline innovative ideas related to teaching and learning. His expectation is that some of the teachers in the reading group will eventually design coursework based on the theories about which they are reading. Guberman plans to form a group to read Andrew Whitworth's (2014) *Radical Information Literacy: Reclaiming the Political Heart of the IL Movement.* The most important criterion for selecting a venue to become involved with in the hopes of advancing an informed learning approach to information literacy is that the teachers participating in it must be interested in improving student learning.

10.4 CONSULTING APPROACHES THAT FOCUS ON CREATING SHARED GOALS

Collaborations between librarians and teachers to integrate information literacy into courses using an informed learning approach must be founded on common goals. Developing common goals was the aim of the librarians involved in the IMPACT program when working with teachers to make their classrooms more student-centered or to bring information literacy into courses (Flierl et al., 2016). As educators, academic librarians may have strong views about what is important for students to learn about using information to be successful in their courses and their various undertakings after they leave their college or university. Therefore, librarians may feel that it is hard to develop shared goals with teachers, who ultimately decide what changes are made to coursework. It may be more difficult in cases when a librarian or teacher emphasizes a situated or critical understanding of teaching and learning that does not resonate with their partner's view of what is important for students to learn. While it is not essential to agree on all the specifics, both the librarian and the teacher must be able to come to consensus on key aspects of the coursework designed through the collaboration.

Integrating information literacy using an informed learning approach requires that goals for learning align with some or all of the principles and characteristics of the informed learning model developed by Bruce (2008). Through their collaboration, the teacher and the librarian must agree as to how students need to use information to learn in the learning environment they are cocreating. Recognizing that teaching, learning, and information literacy are related (Bruce, Edwards, & Lupton, 2006), it is essential that teachers and librarians working together comprehend each other's views. Academic librarians and teachers engaged in a collaboration must negotiate how their perspectives will be represented in the course they are codesigning. The librarians involved in the IMPACT program, all of whom have worked closely with teachers in other contexts, recognize that teachers trying to improve learning in their course are more likely to be open to new ideas.

Developing courses to improve student learning will not always involve information literacy. While the librarians participating in the

IMPACT program worked with such courses, they were also often able to suggest ways that intentionally using information could enhance the learning of course content. The importance of recognizing that there are multiple views of information literacy cannot be overstated. If a teacher is resistant to an idea for having students learn to use information in their course, it may be that the idea does not fit into the teacher's view of information literacy. If a teacher considers it as a new content that needs to be taught separately from course content (Webber & Johnston, 2005), they may not be open to discussing how information literacy should be addressed in the context of learning about a discipline or profession. Encountering resistance does not necessarily suggest that a librarian should offer information literacy solutions that align precisely with the teacher's views. However, the librarian will need to be strategic in how they work with that teacher. To the degree possible, librarians may attempt to work with these teachers to help them see the role of information literacy in fostering student learning.

Academic librarians working with teachers to integrate information literacy into courses using an informed learning approach are engaged in similar activities to instructional developers working with teachers in other ways to enhance student learning. Success in integrating information literacy into coursework using an informed learning approach begins with conversation. Librarians need to know what teachers are trying to achieve in their courses. As suggested by Flierl and his colleagues (2016), librarians should begin by asking what teachers want their students "to know, do, or value" at the end of the course, before asking them how students use information to accomplish these goals. Does the teacher want to prepare students for the workplace, or open their eyes to injustice? The answers to such questions frame how students need to engage with information in the learning context.

10.5 CONCLUSION

Academic librarians have the opportunity to extend their contribution to student learning in a significant and meaningful way. However, doing this means that they have to reorient part of their information literacy efforts to find places where they can influence how students use information as they are learning. This chapter outlined three essential things that are necessary for applying an informed learning approach to integrating information literacy into courses. Academic librarians must recognize the relationship between using information and learning (Limberg, 2000; Lupton, 2008; Maybee, Bruce, et al., 2017), which may be significant for developing effective teaching in which students use information within a broader learning context.

Librarians working in higher education also need to locate the teachers on their campuses that are interested in teaching and learning innovations, and whom may therefore be open to an informed learning approach. In working with teachers interested in improving teaching and learning, academic librarians must utilize a consulting approach that allows for the creation of shared goals for student learning that include learning about using information as well as course content. Chapter 11 focuses on how academic librarians can leverage their existing skills to advance informed learning, but may also benefit by becoming aware of emerging approaches to information literacy, learning more about teaching and learning theories and models, and further developing their consulting abilities.

REFERENCES

ACRL. (2000). *Information literacy competency standards for higher education*. Chicago, IL: Association of College and Research Libraries.
ACRL. (2015). Framework for information literacy for higher education. Association of College and Research Libraries. Retrieved from http://www.ala.org/acrl/standards/ilframework.
Bruce, C. S. (2008). *Informed learning*. Chicago, IL: American Library Association.
Bruce, C. S., Edwards, S. L., & Lupton, M. (2006). Six frames for information literacy education: A conceptual framework for interpreting the relationships between theory and practice. *ITALICS (Innovations in Teaching and Learning Information and Computer Science), 51*(1), 1–18.
Flierl, M., Maybee, C., Riehle, C. F., & Johnson, N. (2016). IMPACT lessons: Strategically embedding MIL through teacher development in higher education. In D. Oberg & S. Ingvaldsen (Eds.), *Media and information literacy in higher education* (pp. 119–133). Oxford: Chandos.
Kapitzke, C. (2003). Information literacy: A review and poststructural critique. *Australian Journal of Language and Literacy, 26*(1), 53–66.
Kari, J., & Savolainen, R. (2010). In A. Lloyd & S. Talja (Eds.), *On the connections between information use and learning process* (pp. 229–249). Wagga Wagga, Australia: Charles Sturt University, Centre for Information Studies.

Limberg, L. (1999). Experiencing information seeking and learning: A study of the interaction between two phenomena. Information Research, 5(1). Retrieved from http://informationr.net/ir/5-1/paper68.html.

Limberg, L. (2000). Is there a relationship between information seeking and learning outcomes? In Information literacy around the world: Advances in programs and research (pp. 193–207). Wagga Wagga, N.S.W: Charles Sturt University, Centre for Information Studies.

Lloyd, A. (2007). Learning to put out the red stuff: Becoming information literate through discursive practice. *The Library Quarterly*, 77(2), 181–198. https://doi.org/10.1086/517844.

Lloyd, A. (2010). *Information literacy landscapes: Information literacy in education, workplace and everyday contexts.* Oxford: Chandos.

Lupton, M. (2008). *Information literacy and learning.* Blackwood, S. Aust.: Auslib Press.

Maybee, C., Bruce, C. S., Lupton, M., & Rebmann, K. (2017). Designing rich information experiences to shape learning outcomes. *Studies in Higher Education*, 42(12), 2373–2388.

Maybee, C., Doan, T., & Flierl, M. (2016). Information literacy in the active learning classroom. *Journal of Academic Librarianship*, 42(6), 705–711.

Millet, M. S., Donald, J., & Wilson, D. W. (2009). Information literacy across the curriculum: Expanding horizons. *College & Undergraduate Libraries*, 16(2–3), 180–193. https://doi.org/10.1080/10691310902976451.

Pawley, C. (2003). Information literacy: A contradictory coupling. *The Library Quarterly*, 73(4), 422–452.

Simmons, M. H. (2005). Librarians as disciplinary discourse mediators: using genre theory to move toward critical information literacy. *Portal: Libraries & the Academy*, 5(3), 297–311.

Tewell, E. (2015). A decade of critical information literacy: A review of the literature. *Communications in Information Literacy*, 9(1), 24–43.

Webber, S., Boon, S., & Johnston, B. (2005). A comparison of UK academics' conceptions of information literacy in two disciplines: English and marketing. *Library and Information Research*, 29(93), 4–15.

Webber, S., & Johnston, B. (2005). Information literacy in the curriculum: Selected findings from a phenomenographic study of UK conceptions of, and pedagogy for, information literacy. In C. Rust (Ed.), *Improving student learning: Diversity and inclusivity. Proceedings of the 11th ISL Symposium.* (pp. 212–224). Birmingham: Oxford Brookes Univ.

Whitworth, A. (2014). *Radical information literacy: Reclaiming the political heart of the IL movement.* Burlington: Elsevier Science.

CHAPTER 11

Developing Librarians to Support Learning Initiatives

Contents

Abstract

This chapter discusses the knowledge and abilities academic librarians need to have in order to adopt an informed learning approach to integrating information literacy into courses through collaboration with higher education teachers. The knowledge and abilities that academic librarians have developed and use in their current information literacy work may have prepared them for this change. However, there are things which librarians may need to learn more about in order to advance an informed learning approach. To advance informed learning, academic librarians must have communication skills, as well as be knowledgeable about informed learning, other ideas about information literacy, and teaching and learning innovations.

Keywords: Academic librarian development, Professional development, Librarian development gaps, Consulting role of academic librarians, Librarian and teacher collaboration.

11.1 INTRODUCTION

Adopting an informed learning approach to integrating information literacy into college or university courses would be likely to cause a change in which academic librarians would spend more time working

145

with teachers and less time on other instructional duties. Fortunately, the knowledge and abilities that are typically developed and used in the work of many academic librarians have prepared them for this change. Nevertheless, there are things which librarians may need to learn more about in order to advance an informed learning approach. In addition to being knowledgeable about various ideas related to information literacy, academic librarians working to integrate information literacy into courses using an informed learning approach must also be able to collaborate with teachers. In many ways, such collaborations require librarians to adopt a role similar to that of instructional developers, who work with teachers to advance innovative approaches to teaching and learning on their campuses.

Instructional developers need to be knowledgeable regarding teaching and learning ideas, including pedagogical strategies and assessment (Gillespie, Robertson, & Bergquist, 2010). Academic librarians may be familiar with pedagogic ideas that they have used in their teaching; however, they may need to become familiar with the various ideas about teaching and learning used by a teacher with whom they collaborate. Instructional developers do much of their work through consulting and collaboration, which requires communication skills, but also a broader understanding of institutional goals and culture, such as the relationship between teaching and learning and tenure and promotion requirements (Gillespie et al., 2010). Academic librarians are often known for their ability to work across departmental and other common academic boundaries. Adopting an informed learning approach necessitates that librarians hone their communication skills to be effective in persuading teachers to make changes that allow students to learn to use information as part of the learning outcomes for their course.

11.2 REQUIRED KNOWLEDGE AND ABILITIES

The knowledge and abilities necessary for academic librarians to adopt an informed learning approach to integrating information literacy into courses on their campuses may overlap with things they have learned in their practice as librarians and information literacy teachers. Library and information science programs tend not offer many courses related to information literacy or teaching

(Hensley, 2015; Julien, 2005; Sproles, Johnson, & Farison, 2008). Therefore, it is likely that academic librarians' knowledge and abilities related to teaching and learning may vary widely and will need to be expanded. Certainly, academic librarians new to the profession will need to develop their skill-set. To further informed learning on their campuses, academic librarians need to be knowledgeable about informed learning, other ideas about information literacy, and teaching and learning. They must also have the communication skills and institutional support, such as time, to be able to engage in collaboration.

11.2.1 Informed Learning

Informed learning is a different approach to information literacy than that which is typically practiced in higher education. It may prove challenging for academic librarians to shift their practices to focus on developing learning environments in which students learn to use information as they engage with course content. Librarians must understand the key aspects of informed learning deeply enough that they can apply it in their work with teachers and others to develop informed learning activities and assignments. The central concept of informed learning is that students must use information to learn (Bruce, 2008). Using it in the context of academic learning will prepare students to use information to learn in their various roles as professionals, citizens, parents, and so forth, after leaving the university.

As outlined previously, informed learning is grounded in the three principles of (1) building on learners' current experiences, (2) promoting simultaneous learning about course content and using information, and (3) enabling learners to experience both using information and subject content in new ways (Bruce & Hughes, 2010). Informed learning is also associated with several characteristics. One characteristic of informed learning is that it is developed through collaboration with teachers, librarians, and others, such as information technologists. Information practices are typically drawn from disciplinary or professional practices. What is considered "information" depends on the context, but can be anything that is informing (Bruce, 2008). Therefore, information may include the textual forms of information, such as articles, books, and so forth, typically used in academia, but it may also include visual, auditory, or embodied sources. Informed learning usually involves active learning in which students actively engage with, analyze, and interpret information to learn. Informed learning also aims to foster transformative experiences in which students change their understandings of themselves, their discipline, or their professional practice as a result of instruction.

The principles outlined by Bruce (2008) are the essential elements of informed learning. While the characteristics she outlines are important as well, it is not necessary that all informed learning environments include each of the characteristics. For example, the vignettes in Chapter 7 illustrate learning environments and assignments that display some, but not all, of the characteristics of informed learning. In their work with teachers to integrate information literacy into courses using an informed learning approach, academic librarians need to be able to determine which aspects of informed learning are crucial for enabling students to learn to use information as they engage with course content. Making such decisions requires a thorough understanding of informed learning. This book provides a primer for informed learning. Academic librarians intending to use informed learning in their practice may wish to study the scholarship on it (e.g., Bruce, 2008; Bruce & Hughes, 2010; Bruce, Hughes, & Somerville, 2012). Librarians may also find it useful to investigate the related literature on students' experiences of using information (e.g., Andretta, 2012; Diehm & Lupton, 2012; Lupton, 2008; Maybee, 2007).

11.2.2 Information Literacy

When working to integrate information literacy into a course using an informed learning approach, an academic librarian may need to be aware of the teacher's view of information literacy. Teachers may not be explicitly aware of their view of information literacy. Nevertheless, they will have an understanding of it. Knowledge of different ways in which information literacy is understood will aid academic librarians in recognizing the way in which a teacher conceptualizes information literacy. This awareness will allow the librarian to work with the view put forth by the teacher, or to adopt strategies aimed at persuading the teacher to change their approach.

Academic librarians may already be knowledgeable of various approaches to information literacy. For example, they may be familiar with critical information literacy through its growing body of scholarship. Academic librarians in the United States are likely to be familiar with the conceptualization of information literacy offered by ACRL's (2015) *Framework for Information Literacy for Higher Education*. The *Six Frames* model developed by Bruce, Edwards, and Lupton (2006), which aligns views of information literacy with views of teaching and learning, provides a framework for broadly identifying a teacher's view of information literacy. Nevertheless, academic librarians may find it useful to stay abreast of new ideas about information literacy that emerge through scholarship. Ideas encountered in information literacy scholarship may be helpful when considering informed learning. For example, Lloyd's findings revealing how professionals, such as firefighters and nurses, use bodily information to make decisions (Bonner & Lloyd, 2011; Lloyd, 2007) has implications when considering what counts as information when developing informed learning experiences for students.

11.2.3 Teaching And Learning

Academic librarians need to work with teachers and may often be involved in educational initiatives on their campuses to advance informed learning. Therefore, it is essential that they are knowledgeable about teaching and learning innovations on their campuses. Many librarians may be familiar with different pedagogic techniques and other educational ideas from their work as teachers. However, librarians typically do not learn about teaching in a systematic way (Walter, 2006). A study of Canadian librarians revealed that they prepare for and improve their teaching through on-the-job experience, reading professional literature, and attending workshops (Julien & Genuis, 2011). The experience of Canadian librarians taking informal approaches to learn about teaching and learning is likely to be similar for librarians in other parts of the world as well.

The librarians participating in the Instruction Matters: Purdue Academic Course Transformation (IMPACT) program learn about teaching and learning through their involvement in the program. The librarians selected to participate in IMPACT had teaching experience gained through their roles as departmental liaisons, and participation in development opportunities intended to enhance their teaching skills. Several of the librarians had attended the teacher or programming tracks of ACRL's Immersion Program, in which attendees learn about different learning theories, as well as classroom and assessment techniques. Nevertheless, they were exposed to many new educational ideas and theories during the weekly IMPACT FLC meetings. When new educational concepts are introduced into the FLC by the IMPACT management team, the librarians, CIE, and ITaP staff discuss their characteristics and how they may be useful in a redesigned course. The knowledge gained through participation in the IMPACT program is used to coach teachers in making their course more student-centered.

Perhaps more important than being broadly conversant with emerging ideas about teaching and learning, academic librarians must be able to work with such ideas when they encounter them. As with the librarians involved in IMPACT, academic librarians advancing informed learning on their campuses are likely to work in an environment in which educational theories and models are being discussed and applied to curricula. It is necessary to be able to align informed learning with other educational ideas. Maybee and Flierl were able to draw informed learning together with other theories used in the IMPACT program. Their efforts guided their work with the teachers in the program, but also allowed them to share with the library and information science community how informed learning could be further developed by drawing it together with self-determination theory (Maybee & Flierl, 2017) and backward design (Bruce et al., 2017).

As discussed in Chapter 5, instructional design can be a useful tool as it provides structure for working with teachers to design coursework. Instructional design is a necessary skill-set for librarians involved in teaching and designing assignments (ACRL, 2007). However, librarians are not typically introduced to instructional design during their education (Hensley, 2015). In some cases, librarians may be able to work with instructional developers at their institutions (Clapp, Johnson, Schwieder, & Craig, 2013), or some academic libraries may hire instructional design librarians dedicated to supporting teaching efforts (Shank, 2006). Despite programs such as ACRL's (2013) Immersion, which foster academic librarians' teaching and design abilities, there remains a concern in librarianship that not all librarians engage in a formal approach when designing learning activities (e.g., Davis, 2013; Hensley, 2015; Summey, 2013). Instructional design models, such as backward design with its emphasis on learning outcomes, assessment instruments, and learning activities (Wiggins & McTighe, 2005), highlight key elements of a course that can be the focus of planning discussions between classroom faculty and librarians.

Academic librarians working with teachers to integrate information literacy using an informed learning approach will also have to make suggestions regarding how information use will be assessed. From an informed learning perspective, assessment must measure student learning of both information use and course content. In an informed learning environment, students are actively using information to learn about course content. Although it might be possible to do so, it is unlikely that testing would reflect students' ability to use information in new ways. Academic librarians working with teachers to create informed learning assessment should be prepared to suggest strategies that reveal students facility with using, as well as their awareness of how they engage with, information.

11.2.4 Collaboration

There are many articles in the literature about librarians' collaboration with disciplinary teachers. Predominately, these articles describe embedding information literacy into courses in ways that align with the ACRL (2000) *Information Literacy Competency Standards for Higher Education*. Thus, they are not examples of collaborations to integrate information literacy into courses that have students learn course content by engaging with information. The collaborative process to design informed learning requires that the librarian have a thorough understanding of the teachers' goals for learning and that the teacher comes to understand how using information in particular ways may foster content-focused learning goals. Academic librarians working with teachers to integrate information literacy into courses using an informed learning approach must be able to communicate ideas about informed learning. They must also be able to suggest learning activities in which students learn about course content as they learn about and practice using information.

Developing collaborations often begins with building relationships. As with instructional developers (Gillespie et al., 2010), academic librarians should make it a point to learn about the teaching cultures on their campuses, including how teaching and learning are construed in tenure and promotion policies. How much time a teacher is willing to contribute to a teaching and learning effort may depend on how it supports their attaining tenure or promotion. Librarians may also want to investigate how teaching and learning are supported by the department of the teacher with which they want to work. When working one-on-one, it is important that librarians and teachers can develop shared goals for their collaborative efforts (Flierl, Maybee, Riehle, & Johnson, 2016). From an informed learning perspective, shared goals will likely center around how content-focused learning goals can be achieved by having students use information in particular ways. Collaborating in this way requires excellent communication skills. Mentioned previously, the librarians working with IMPACT identified instructional design as a tool that may be of use in such a situation by providing a common language and a structure for discussing potential changes to aspects of a course.

11.3 DEVELOPMENT GAPS

Academic librarians should conduct a needs assessment to determine their gaps in the knowledge and abilities needed to partner with others to integrate information literacy into courses using an informed learning approach. The needs assessment should focus on identifying the knowledge and abilities required to advance informed learning:

- Informed learning—developing a thorough understanding of the principles and characteristics and experience participating in designing instruction using the model,
- Information literacy—keeping abreast of current trends with an eye towards drawing applicable ideas into informed learning.
- Teaching and learning—understanding teaching and learning theories and models and how they may align with informed learning, instructional design models, and assessment practices for measuring students' learning related to using information as well as course content.
- Collaboration—developing excellent communication skills that may be used to cultivate shared goals with teachers centered on the advancement of content-focused learning through engagement with information.

Once identified, academic librarians can work to the fill gaps and round out their professional knowledge and abilities. For those in positions responsible for the development of other academic librarians, the needs assessment should include all librarians engaged in partnering with teachers, and plans should be put in place to provide librarians with development opportunities.

11.4 EXISTING OPPORTUNITIES FOR DEVELOPMENT

Academic libraries need to provide development opportunities for their librarians that support their collaborative role in working with teachers to advance informed learning. As with teaching (Julien & Genuis, 2011), academic librarians are likely to learn knowledge and abilities that support advancing informed learning through on-the-job experience, reading professional literature, and attending workshops. When possible, academic librarians can be supported in their consultative roles through mentorship by librarians with more experience partnering with teachers to develop coursework. Experienced librarians may also be called on to give presentations and lead discussions about their collaborative work. As we have done at Purdue, academic librarians may form a reading group and read and discuss articles about informed learning and other educational theories and models.

Academic libraries should also take advantage of regional and national programs that aim to develop librarians in their teaching and design roles. Of the various programs available from which to choose, many academic librarians in the United States attend the Immersion Program hosted by ACRL. The Immersion program brings together a group of academic librarians to learn about information literacy and teaching and learning. Participants are encouraged to consider ways of improving their information literacy practice when they return to their institutions. The primary foci of the Immersion program are on developing librarians as teachers and on supporting them to advance information literacy programmatic efforts. Although it does not directly focus on the collaborative aspects of information literacy work, the ideas about information literacy, teaching and learning, and instructional design that librarians learn about through participation in the Immersion Program are relevant background knowledge that may be applicable when using an informed learning approach. For example, Purdue librarians who have attended Immersion have relayed that it helped them to think broadly about some educational ideas that supported their work with teachers in the IMPACT program.

Advancing informed learning involves collaborating with teachers, and thus, academic librarians need to gain an understanding of perspectives on teaching and learning held by teachers and others, such as professional developers and technologists, that influence instructional practice. Therefore, academic librarians should attend professional development activities that focus on teaching and learning beyond librarianship. Librarians should explore and take advantage of the events on their campus. College and university teaching centers typically offer workshops to learn about pedagogic strategies, such as active learning techniques, assessment methods, and so forth. There may also be presentations about specific approaches to teaching and learning by speakers brought to the institution. At a large institution like Purdue, there are a number of teaching and learning workshops and conferences hosted throughout the academic year, which in the past have included events on team-based learning, competency-based learning, highly effective educational practices, writing across the curriculum, among others.

If funding and support are available, academic librarians may attend teaching and learning conferences outside of their institutions. There are many such conferences held all over the world. Conferences that may be particularly relevant to academic librarians' work to integrate information literacy into courses using an informed learning approach are those attended by professional developers. In the United States, such a conference is hosted by the Professional Organizational Development (POD) Network. The POD conference focuses on the scholarship of teaching, learning, and organizational development (POD Network, 2017). The conference is attended by approximately 1000 instructional developers and higher education teachers each year. While the presentations at the POD conference cover a wide array of teaching and learning topics, many sessions offer techniques and strategies for working with teachers to improve courses.

11.5 CONCLUSION

This chapter discussed the skill-set needed by academic librarians to advance informed learning through collaborations with teachers on their campuses. As academic librarians identify gaps in their knowledge and abilities, they can engage in various development opportunities to support their informed learning practice. Chapter 12 concludes the book by discussing the development of a design model for informed learning, and the benefits of classroom research to investigate informed learning efforts in higher education.

REFERENCES

ACRL. (2000). *Information literacy competency standards for higher education*. Chicago, IL: Association of College and Research Libraries.

ACRL. (2007). *Association of College and Research Libraries standards for proficiencies for instruction librarians and coordinators*. Retrieved from http://www.ala.org/acrl/standards/profstandards (12 December 2016).

ACRL. (2013). *Immersion teacher track: Individual development for instruction skills*. Retrieved from http://www.ala.org/acrl/immersion/teachertrack (13 December 2016).

ACRL. (2015). *Framework for information literacy for higher education*. Association of College and Research Libraries. Retrieved from http://www.ala.org/acrl/standards/ilframework.

Andretta, S. (2012). *Ways of experiencing information literacy: Making the case for a relational approach*. Oxford: Chandos Pub.

Bonner, A., & Lloyd, A. (2011). What information counts at the moment of practice? Information practices of renal nurses. *Journal of Advanced Nursing*, *67*(6), 1213–1221. https://doi.org/10.1111/j.1365-2648.2011.05613.x.

Bruce, C. S. (2008). *Informed learning*. Chicago, IL: American Library Association.

Bruce, C. S., Demasson, A., Hughes, H., Lupton, M., Sayyad Abdi, E., Maybee, C., et al. (2017). Information literacy and informed learning: Conceptual innovations for IL research and practice futures. *Journal of Information Literacy*, *11*(1), 4–22. https://doi.org/10.11645/11.1.2184.

Bruce, C. S., Edwards, S. L., & Lupton, M. (2006). Six frames for information literacy education: A conceptual framework for interpreting the relationships between theory and practice. *ITALICS (Innovations in Teaching and Learning Information and Computer Science)*, *51*(1), 1–18.

Bruce, C. S., & Hughes, H. (2010). Informed learning: A pedagogical construct for information literacy. *Library and Information Science Research*, *32*(4), A2–A8.

Bruce, C. S., Hughes, H., & Somerville, M. (2012). Supporting informed learners in the 21st century. *Library Trends*, *61*(3), 522–545.

Clapp, M., Johnson, M., Schwieder, D., & Craig, C. (2013). Innovation in the academy: Creating an online information literacy course. *Journal of Library & Information Services in Distance Learning*, *7*(3), 247–263. https://doi.org/10.1080/1533290X.2013.805663.

Davis, A. L. (2013). Using instructional design principles to develop effective information literacy instruction: The ADDIE model. *College and Research Libraries News*, *74*(4), 205–207.

Diehm, R.-A., & Lupton, M. (2012). Approaches to learning information literacy: A phenomenographic study. *The Journal of Academic Librarianship*, *38*(4), 217–225.

Flierl, M., Maybee, C., Riehle, C. F., & Johnson, N. (2016). IMPACT lessons: Strategically embedding MIL through teacher development in higher education. In D. Oberg & S. Ingvaldsen (Eds.), *Media and information literacy in higher education* (pp. 119–133). Oxford: Chandos.

Gillespie, K. J., Robertson, D. L., & Bergquist, W. H. (2010). Important skills and knowledge. In *A guide to faculty development: Practical advice, examples, and resources* (2nd ed., pp. 83–98). Hoboken, NJ: John Wiley & Sons, Inc.

Hensley, M. (2015). Improving LIS education in teaching librarians to teach. In D. Mueller (Ed.), *ACRL 2015 Proceedings* (pp. 315–322). Chicago, IL: Association of College and Research Libraries. Retrieved from http://www.ala.org/acrl/sites/ala.org.acrl/files/content/conferences/confsandpreconfs/2015/Hensley.pdf.

Julien, H. (2005). Education for information literacy instruction: A global perspective. *Journal of Education for Library and Information Science, 46*(3), 210–216. https://doi.org/10.2307/40323845.

Julien, H., & Genuis, S. K. (2011). Librarians' experiences of the teaching role: A national survey of librarians. *Library and Information Science Research, 33*(2), 103–111. https://doi.org/10.1016/j.lisr.2010.09.005.

Lloyd, A. (2007). Learning to put out the red stuff: Becoming information literate through discursive practice. *The Library Quarterly, 77*(2), 181–198. https://doi.org/10.1086/517844.

Lupton, M. (2008). Evidence, argument and social responsibility: First-year students' experiences of information literacy when researching an essay. *Higher Education Research & Development, 27*(4), 399–414.

Maybee, C. (2007). Understanding our student learners: A phenomenographic study revealing the ways that undergraduate women at Mills College understand using information. *Reference Services Review, 35*(3), 452–462.

Maybee, C., & Flierl, M. (2017). Motivating learners through information literacy. In S. Kurbanoğlu, J. Boustany, S. Špiranec, E. Grassian, D. Mizrachi, L. Roy, & T. Çakmak (Eds.), *Information literacy in the inclusive society (communications in computer and information science series). Proceedings of the 4th European information literacy conference* (pp. 698–707). Heidelberg: Springer.

POD Network. (2017). *2017 POD Network conference.* Retrieved from http://pod-network.org/event/2017-pod-network-conference/#overviewmission (17 July 2017).

Shank, J. (2006). The blended librarian: A job announcement analysis of the newly emerging position of instructional design librarian. *College & Research Libraries, 67*(6), 514–524.

Sproles, C., Johnson, A., & Farison, L. (2008). What the teachers are teaching: How MLIS programs are preparing academic librarians for instructional roles. *Journal of Education for Library and Information Science, 49*(3), 195–209.

Summey, T. P. (2013). But we don't have an instructional designer: Designing online library instruction using ISD techniques. *Journal of Library & Information Services in Distance Learning, 7*(1/2), 169–183. https://doi.org/10.1080/1533290X.2012.705630.

Walter, S. (2006). Instructional improvement: Building capacity for the professional development of librarians as teachers. *Reference & User Services Quarterly, 45*(3), 213–218.

Wiggins, G. P., & McTighe, J. (2005). *Understanding by design* (2nd ed.). Alexandria, VA: Association for Supervision and Curriculum Development.

CHAPTER 12

The Way Forward

Contents

Abstract

This chapter concludes the book by affirming the importance of academic libraries adopting an informed learning approach to integrating information literacy, and highlighting informed learning design as an instructional design process for developing courses that are guided by an informed learning approach. Academic librarians using an informed learning approach in their practice may view themselves as joining a community of scholars and practitioners also interested in this approach to information literacy. These librarians are encouraged to adopt a scholarly approach to the implementation of informed learning in higher education settings and share the results of their investigations through peer-reviewed publication.

Keywords: Informed learning community, Informed learning design, Instructional design, Informed learning research, Information literacy research.

12.1 INTRODUCTION

There are many benefits to utilizing an informed learning approach in higher education. Chief among those benefits is that student learning can be shaped and enhanced by academic librarians and teachers being intentional about how students engage with information (Maybee, Bruce, Lupton, & Rebmann, 2017). Despite the benefits, academic librarians may face challenges when adopting an informed learning approach to integrating information literacy for the first time. In this chapter, a forthcoming instructional design tool, called

IMPACT Learning
https://doi.org/10.1016/B978-0-08-102077-7.00012-4
157

informed learning design, is highlighted that will provide a process and targets for discussing informed learning with teachers.

To conclude the book, one final suggestion is made. As academic librarians draw informed learning into their practice, they are joining a community of scholars and practitioners also interested in this approach to information literacy. Academic librarians adopting an informed learning approach are encouraged to participate in future research by taking a scholarly approach to the development of informed learning coursework and publishing the outcomes of such projects. Collectively sharing knowledge learned through the implementation of informed learning in higher education settings will further our ability to address the information literacy needs of higher education students.

12.2 INFORMED LEARNING AND HIGHER EDUCATION

This book has discussed various aspects of an informed learning approach to integrating information literacy into courses and provided examples of how the approach has been applied in a university setting. The description of informed learning, which encompassed outlining its principles and characteristics, was intended to provide academic librarians with an overall understanding of the approach and its applicability in higher education. The discussion and the examples recounting how the librarians used the approach in their work with teachers in the IMPACT program at Purdue was intended to provide a realistic picture of the opportunities and challenges of applying an informed learning approach in practice in a higher education setting. Having examined informed learning broadly, and its application in one higher education content in detail, this chapter will conclude the discussion by reiterating three closely related goals that academic libraries may accomplish by adopting an informed learning approach to integrating information literacy on their campuses.

First, adopting an informed learning approach to integrate information literacy into courses by partnering with educational initiatives on campus will align an academic library's mission for information literacy with their institution's goals for student learning. One key to reaching this goal is to identify educational initiatives that are intended to help the institution achieve a goal for teaching and learning. The application of an informed learning approach will allow for the integration of information literacy in a way that furthers the learning goals of the initiative, thus highlighting for stakeholders the value of information literacy.

Second, adopting an informed learning approach aligns information literacy efforts with teachers' goals for learning within a course. Informed learning is different than the information skills approach with which many teachers may be familiar. The information skills approach results in academic librarians teaching students a variety of skills, such as developing search terms, using Boolean operators, and evaluating information using generic checklists of criteria. While these skills may be valuable, they do not directly influence content-focused learning outcomes as an informed learning approach has been shown to do (Maybee et al., 2017). Therefore, it may be hard for teachers (and students) to see the relevance of such skills when they are divorced from the disciplinary content the students enrolled in a course to learn about, such as engineering concepts, women's studies theories, or nursing practices. An informed learning approach bridges this gap by focusing on advancing content-focused learning outcomes through the intentional use of information.

Higher education teachers may also have situated or critical goals for student learning that are not addressed by an information skills approach. For example, a teacher may have a situated goal of students shifting their identity towards that of a professional practitioner. Using an informed learning approach, academic librarians can help enable students to use information as a practitioner would, such as analyzing data as would a political scientist, or communicating complex information to patients as would a nutritionist. Academic librarians can also apply an informed learning approach when working with teachers whose goals for learning are underpinned by a critical perspective by helping make connections between information production and use and the broader cultural, social, and political concerns the students are learning about in their courses. Addressing the situated and critical aspects of information literacy in higher education curricula is crucial to adequately preparing students to use information to learn and to take action in their future lives as students, professionals, citizens, and so forth.

The third, and most important of the goals, is that by working with teachers to integrate information literacy into courses using an informed learning approach, academic librarians are enabling students to use information to learn. Informed learning encourages the creation of authentic learning activities that allow students to engage with information as they do in their various endeavors outside of the academia. When appropriate, informed learning advocates for introducing students to disciplinary and professional information practices such as those they may encounter in their future careers (Bruce & Hughes, 2010). However, just as in daily life, information can be anything that is informing, such as a memo, a picture, data, or points gleaned through discussion (Bruce, 2008). With its emphasis on learning to use information in different contexts, informed learning is associated with life-long learning in which students may continue to use information to learn new things throughout their lives (Bruce, Hughes, & Somerville, 2012). That is to say, students who have experienced intentionally using information to learn in college are more likely to be prepared to use information to learn and grow in their endeavors after college.

12.3 INFORMED LEARNING DESIGN

To advance informed learning, academic librarians need to do three things. First, they must view learning as the outcome of using information. Second, they have to find teachers on their campuses willing to work with them to integrate information literacy into courses using an informed learning approach. Finally, academic librarians need to be able to consult and collaborate with teachers. As discussed previously, instructional design can be an aid to librarians in their efforts to work with teachers to integrate information literacy into higher education courses using an informed learning approach. Instructional design models offer a process and a specific target, such as learning outcomes, assessment, and learning activities, which provides a focus for collaborative work. Discussed in Chapter 8, a new design model, called informed learning design, is being developed specifically to guide the design of elements of informed learning courses (Bruce et al., 2017).

Informed learning design was specifically created to support the advancement of informed learning as an approach to integrating information literacy into courses in higher education. The design model is grounded in the variation theory of learning, which argues that learning is becoming aware of aspects of something of which one was previously unaware (Marton, 2014; Marton, Runesson, & Tsui, 2004). Informed learning and the variation theory of learning emerged from the same research trajectory that began by investigating how students' experience the various phenomena about which they are learning (see Marton, Hounsell, & Entwistle, 1997). From an informed learning perspective, teaching efforts should endeavor to enable students to become aware of aspects related to both using information and course content.

Drawing from the structural elements of backward design (Wiggins & McTighe, 2005), the three stages of informed learning design are (1) identifying learning related to using information and course content, (2) defining assessment methods for gauging students' increased awareness of using information and course content, and (3) determining activities that enable students to learn content by intentionally using information (Bruce et al., 2017). In working with teachers to integrate information literacy into courses using an informed learning approach, even if informally, academic librarians may want to follow the three stages of informed learning design. Working with teachers to determine goals for learning that address both using information and course content will help ensure that teachers understand the implications of applying an informed learning approach in the course. The academic librarian and the teacher should consider how goals related to content-focused learning may be influenced by the ways in which students engage with information as they learn (Maybee et al., 2017). The goals identified through the collaborative work of librarians and teachers can then be used as a guide for the identification of assessment instruments and selection of informed learning activities.

Mentioned in Chapter 8, the research team, comprised of Clarence Maybee from Purdue, Christine Bruce and Mandy Lupton from Queensland University of Technology, and Ming Fai Pang from The University of Hong Kong, anticipate publishing a paper in late 2017 that describes informed learning design in greater detail.

12.4 INFORMED LEARNING RESEARCH

Informed learning continues to evolve and grow through further research and practice. Academic librarians adopting an informed learning approach in higher education are a community of practitioners. Ideally, they will find ways to communicate with one another and share ideas and opportunities for advancing informed learning, and also to discuss challenges they face in implementing informed learning in their educational contexts. Academic librarians using an informed learning approach should also consider participating in research to explore elements of teaching and learning in an informed learning environment. Such research would illuminate the effectiveness of an informed learning approach implemented within a specific context, allowing for its refinement. Sharing the results of such research would add to the collective knowledge of informed learning and provide guidance for academic librarians considering adopting an informed learning approach on their campuses.

The use of informed learning design to frame teaching efforts lends itself to a scholarly approach to teaching. First identified by Boyer (1990), scholarly teaching suggests an intentional and structured approach to implementing changes in courses (Smith, 2008). However, academic librarians and teachers may extend their scholarly approach to developing informed learning to create what is termed the "scholarship of teaching and learning" (Richlin, 2001; Smith, 2008). Scholarship of teaching and learning research typically indicates a structured approach to implementing changes in courses in which the outcome of the changes are evaluated and results reported in peer-reviewed publishing venues. In the United States, the scholarship of teaching and learning is typically associated with quantitative research methods. However, informed learning has grown out of the qualitative tradition, which offers different, but no less informative, results.

Academic librarians adopting an informed learning approach when working with teachers to integrate information literacy into courses have an opportunity to investigate informed learning, as a change implemented within the particular teaching and learning context that the project takes place. For example, academic librarians could investigate informed learning in an introductory undergraduate agriculture course in which the students are examining weather change data to determine crop selection in the Mid-west region of the United States, or a graduate education course in which the students collect and analyze syllabi from across the world to identify exemplary teaching practices. Informed learning could also be studied in projects where pedagogic models are employed as well, such as Diekema, Holliday, and Leary's (2011) project to construct an online learning module underpinned by informed learning and problem-based learning. The methods used to investigate informed learning will depend on a number of factors that include the familiarity of the academic librarians conducting the research with particular research methods.

To date, the investigation of informed learning in formal learning environments has primarily used a phenomenographic research approach that compares a teacher's experiences of lessons with students' experiences (Maybee et al., 2017; Maybee, Bruce, Lupton, & Rebmann, 2013; Smeaton, Maybee, Bruce, & Hughes, 2016). Growing out of the same research traditions, one methodology that may be useful for studying informed learning is called learning study (see, e.g., Pang & Marton, 2003). Building from the "lesson study" methods developed in Japan to investigate and improve classroom lessons (Lewis, 2000), learning study has been designed to examine classroom lessons through the lens of variation theory (Marton, 2014; Marton et al., 2004). Learning study research aims to identify the ways in which classroom lessons enable student awareness of aspects of that which they are learning about, such as a concept, theory, or practice. The findings are used to inform the modification of the lessons, and the investigation continues until students are learning as intended by the teacher. Applying learning study methods to an investigation of informed learning activities would involve determining aspects related to what was being learned about course content as well as to using information.

Regardless of the methods, academic librarians integrating information literacy into courses using an informed learning approach should consider conducting research to determine the effectiveness of their efforts in order to improve upon them. For the advancement of informed learning practices, they should also consider sharing their findings through publication with the community of informed learning practitioners and researchers.

12.5 FINAL THOUGHTS

Information literacy efforts in higher education sit at a cross-roads. Academic libraries can continue their efforts to teach students general information skills, or they can take a new approach in which students learn to use information within the context of learning in their courses. As the American poet Robert Frost (1915) suggested in his poem, "The Road Not Taken," it can be difficult to break with convention and head in a new direction. Reaching important goals sometimes requires blazing a new trail. Scholars and practitioners alike are questioning the current information literacy practices in higher education. Informed learning offers a new pathway for developing information literacy efforts that are, to use the words of the poet, "one less traveled by," but that may make "all the difference."

REFERENCES

Boyer, E. L. (1990). *Scholarship reconsidered: Priorities of the professoriate.* Princeton, NJ: The Carnegie Foundation for the Advancement of Teaching.

Bruce, C. S. (2008). *Informed learning.* Chicago, IL: American Library Association.

Bruce, C. S., Demasson, A., Hughes, H., Lupton, M., Sayyad Abdi, E., Maybee, C., et al. (2017). Information literacy and informed learning: Conceptual innovations for IL research and practice futures. *Journal of Information Literacy, 11*(1), 4–22. https://doi.org/10.11645/11.1.2184.

Bruce, C. S., & Hughes, H. (2010). Informed learning: A pedagogical construct for information literacy. *Library and Information Science Research, 32*(4), A2–A8.

Bruce, C. S., Hughes, H., & Somerville, M. (2012). Supporting informed learners in the 21st century. *Library Trends, 61*(3), 522–545.

Diekema, A. R., Holliday, W., & Leary, H. (2011). Re-framing information literacy: Problem-based learning as informed learning. *Library & Information Science Research, 33*(4), 261–268.

Frost, R. (1915). The road not taken. Poetry Foundation. Retrieved from https://www.poetryfoundation.org/poems/44272/the-road-not-taken.

Lewis, C. (2000). *Lesson study: The core of Japanese professional development.* Paper presented at the special interest group on research in mathematics education, American Educational Research Association meeting, New Orleans, April.

Marton, F. (2014). *Necessary conditions for learning.* New York: Routledge.

Marton, F., Hounsell, D., & Entwistle, N. J. (1997). *The experience of learning: Implications for teaching and studying in higher education* (2nd ed.). Edinburgh: Scottish Academic Press.

Marton, F., Runesson, U., & Tsui, A. B. M. (2004). The space of learning. In F. Marton & A. B. M. Tsui (Eds.), *Classroom discourse and the space of learning* (pp. 3–40). Mahwah, NJ: L. Erlbaum Associates.

Maybee, C., Bruce, C. S., Lupton, M., & Rebmann, K. R. (2013). Learning to use information: Informed learning in the undergraduate classroom. *Library & Information Science Research*, *35*(3), 200–206.

Maybee, C., Bruce, C. S., Lupton, M., & Rebmann, K. (2017). Designing rich information experiences to shape learning outcomes. *Studies in Higher Education*, *42*(12), 2373–2388.

Pang, M. F., & Marton, F. (2003). Beyond "Lesson Study": Comparing two ways of facilitating the grasp of some economic concepts. *Instructional Science*, *31*(3), 175–194.

Richlin, L. (2001). Scholarly teaching and the scholarship of teaching. *New Directions for Teaching and Learning*, (86), 57–68.

Smeaton, K., Maybee, C., Bruce, C. S., & Hughes, H. (2016). Expanding literacy and informed learning boundaries with Manga. *ACCESS*, *30*(1), 12–26.

Smith, R. A. (2008). Moving toward the scholarship of teaching and learning: The classroom can be a lab, too! *Teaching of Psychology*, *35*(4), 262–266. https://doi.org/10.1080/00986280802418711.

Wiggins, G. P., & McTighe, J. (2005). *Understanding by design* (2nd ed.). Alexandria, VA: Association for Supervision and Curriculum Development.

INDEX

Note: Page numbers followed by *f* indicate figures and *t* indicate tables.

Printed and bound by CPI Group (UK) Ltd, Croydon, CR0 4YY

08/06/2025

01896869-0010